Mix It Up
WITH COCKTAILS & LIGHT BITES

Massive thank you to: The Hilton Sydney, Australia management, Manuel Prior & The Zeta Bar Team, Sydney, Australia, The White Hart Neutral Bay, Sydney, Australia, Doran Whaite for Cherry Cola recipe, Peter Fischer, Oliver Carpenter and Danny Russo for help on the shoots, Serena Jones and the whole team at barsolutions (www.barsolutions.com.au), Tony Conigliaro, Wayne Collins and Eben Freeman, for untold inspiration, Jim Wood, 8 Track music recordings, London UK. A huge thank you to Micheal and Kym Della Marta in Bronte, Bree Oliver in Tamarama and Andre Brody in Potts Point, Monique Lane and Sophie Collins (my beautiful wife) for all her help and support.

Sources

The Savoy Cocktail Book by Harry Craddock (1938)
Harry's ABC of Mixing Cocktails by Harry MacElhone (1919)
Jerry Thomas's How To Mix Drinks by Jerry Thomas (1862, reprint)
173 Pre-prohibition Cocktails by Tom Bullock and D.J. Frienz (2001)
The Old Waldorf Astoria Bar by A. S. Crocket (1935)

First published in 2014 by New Holland Publishers Pty Ltd
London • Sydney • Auckland

The Chandlery, Unit 009, 50 Westminster Bridge Road, London SE1 7QY, United Kingdom
1/66 Gibbes Street, Chatswood, NSW 2067, Australia
218 Lake Road, Northcote, Auckland, New Zealand

www.newhollandpublishers.com

Copyright © 2014 New Holland Publishers Pty Ltd
Copyright © 2014 in text: Grant Collins
Copyright © 2014 in images: Sue Stubbs

All rights reserved. No part of this publication may be reproduced, stored in a retrieval system or transmitted, in any form or by any means, electronic, mechanical, photocopying, recording or otherwise, without the prior written permission of the publishers and copyright holders.

A record of this book is held at the British Library and the National Library of Australia.

ISBN 9781742575995

Managing director: Fiona Schultz
Project editor: Angela Sutherland
Designer: Caryanne Cleevely
Group production director: Olga Dementiev
Printer: Toppan Leefung Printing Ltd

10 9 8 7 6 5 4 3 2 1

Keep up with New Holland Publishers on Facebook
www.facebook.com/NewHollandPublishers

Mix It Up
WITH COCKTAILS & LIGHT BITES

GRANT COLLINS

Photography by Sue Stubbs

About the author

Grant is the founder and Managing Director of cutting edge international bar consultancy company barsolutions. Grant started his career in the US before returning to his native London to manage the hip Zander Bar which earned 'London Cocktail Bar Of The Year 2000' and himself the prestigious title of 'UK Bar Manager of the Year' 2001.

Discovering the allure of the Sydney lifestyle after a brief holiday, Grant took over as Bar Manager at the newly opened Water Bar at the W Hotel in Woolloomooloo in 2001. Incredibly, Grant's passion and drive for cocktail creation led him to receiving 18 awards on behalf of the Water Bar in a little under five years.

While at Water Bar, Grant's flair and originality in cocktail creation attracted a loyal following at the Water Bar, eager for a taste of the Grant Collins experience. Water Bar went on to win 16 awards under Grants reign from 2001-2005, including the prestigious 'One of the Top 10 Bars in the World' in 2005 by Conde Nast Traveler.

This vast experience and industry recognition saw the formation of Grant's barsolutions consultancy company. Under this banner, Grant consults with many boutique brands including Moet-Hennessy, assisting in the marketing of their vast range of luxury liquor products and public speaking seminars and industry training. In 2005, Grant was head-hunted to open the hottest new bar in Australia, Zeta at Hilton Sydney. He was pivotal in leading them to be awarded 'Australian Liquor Industry's Best New Bar 2005', and 'AHA Cocktail bar of theYear 2006' within its first year of opening. Recently Zeta Bar was awarded 'Cocktail list of the year' 2006 and 2007' by bartender magazine as well as being voted AHA's 'Hotel Cocktail Bar of the year' in 2007, 2008 and 2009, also being nominated as 'One Of The Hottest Bars in the Southern Hemisphere' by Conde Nast Traveler. Zeta has now collected an astonishing 18 key awards in a little over 4 years and is the most decorated Cocktail Bar in Australian Bar history.

Grant has consulted all over the world, bringing with it global recognition. Working in the US, Bali, China, Japan, India, Singapore, Thailand, as well as setting up the hip new Lotus Bar in Hong Kong which has opened to rave reviews, Grant also designed the new bars and cocktail lists for the multi-award winning Ku-De-Ta in Bali, including winning 'Cocktail Bar of the Year' at the Yak awards 2008.

In 2009 Grant was also named as 'One of the World's Greatest Hotel Bartenders' by *Travel & Leisure Magazine* in view of his services to Hotel Bars.

Grant is now one of the most sought after guest speakers and lecturers at industry events and expos such as the London, New York, Sydney and Melbourne Barshows and well as being one of the world's most prominent bar consultants.

He is also currently hosting the newest series of 'Mixing with the Very Best', a show about cocktail culture for the Lifestyle Channel in Australia which has taken him throughout the US and Europe.

About the photographer

Sue Stubbs has been working for over 20 years in photography capturing evocative images of interiors, food, people and gardens. Her clients have included some of the top advertising companies and design agencies as well as Australia's most popular lifestyle magazines such as *Belle*, *Grazia*, *House & Garden*, *Home Beautiful*, *Country Style*, *Green Magazine* and *Sunday Life*. Sue's talent has been recognized internationally, receiving a "Finalist" and "Highly Commended" in the International Garden Photographer (UK) 2009 Competition. She also won the 2004 Horticultural Media Award for best image, and the 2004 Gold Laurel Award. Her photography contribution to *Child* magazine won Gold Front Cover 2013 at the Parenting Media Association awards.

Sue has also photographed titles such as *Sliders*, *Modern Indian*, *Small Fishy Bites*, *Everyday Quinoa*, *A Homegrown Table*, *Superfoods*, and *The Solo Chef* by New Holland Publishers.

Table of Contents

A Brief History

CHAPTER ONE
page 8

The History of Alcohol
The First Cocktail
Prohibition!
Classic Cocktails, 1880–1930

Classics & Twists

CHAPTER TWO
page 68

Tiki Culture
Margarita Madness
Vodka
Creative Cocktails

Progressive & Experimental

CHAPTER THREE
page 114

Experimental and Progressive Cocktails
Chemistry and Cuisine
Layering
Sensory Engagement

CHAPTER FOUR
page 168

Creating Your Very Own Home Bar

Creating Cocktails
Basic Drink-making Techniques
Basic Equipment for your Home Bar
Garnishing your Creations
Simple Drinks Recipes to Create at Home

CHAPTER FIVE
page 254

Food & Cocktails

Modern & Contemporary
History of Tiki Cocktails Culture
Tiki Cocktail Recipes
Contemporary Cocktail History
Modern & Contemporary Classic Recipes

CHAPTER ONE
A Brief History

A Brief History

From its humble beginnings through to its current and more modern incarnations, the cocktail is constantly evolving. This book contains modern and contemporary drinks, as well as how to create simple drinks at home, basic tools required and even how to match drinks with food.

The History of Alcohol

Without alcohol there would be no cocktails. Alcohol can be traced back to 8,000BC and was originally consumed for medicinal purposes rather than for the purpose of simple inebriation. At the time, many did think that a few drinks here or there really did benefit their health as there was no existing benchmarks for its side effects or the consequences of over-indulgence. One of the first people to discover how to distill alcohol (as well as mix simple drinks) was the legendary philosopher Archimedes who used to serve up his 'Elixir's' (loosely translated to 'Water Of Life') to people who were suffering common ailments such as coughs, colds, aches and pains. These simple fixes, which were usually derived from a basic form of distilled liquor (grain was used chiefly at this time), were steeped in herbs and spices that were collected locally, including coriander and rosemary.

As word spread around ancient Greece, many would seek him out for one of his famed potions, which miraculously seemed to 'cure' these sicknesses.

Moving on a few thousand years (2–3,000BC), many in India and Egypt also began distilling. The Indians created a crude beverage known as 'Sura' that was distilled mainly from rice, wheat, sugarcane and grapes. This drink was popular with the peasant population as it was banned by many of the religious sects within the country. It was mainly drunk for its effects rather than the taste, which was rather putrid. The ancient Egyptians were using distilled alcohol in many of their perfumes to preserve the herbs and spices in them, which might have included cinnamon, sandalwood and saffron. These perfumes would not only be used for personal use and hygiene (the Egyptians were notourously obsessed with cleanliness) but, more often than not, for embalming bodies! The Egyptians also distilled beer and wine in smaller quantities for the poor and it was not uncommon for even some wages to be renumerated in beer.

Fast forward to the 5th–10th century and the health problems of alcohol were now becoming quite apparent with liver and stomach issues, as well as gout, pretty commonplace. The crude and often homemade liquor being made was definitely not for the sophisticated palate. Eventually restrictions were enforced in China and Greece, as well as many other parts of Europe, taxing the production of alcohol or controlling the quantities readily available.

In the 10th century, the Italians began fermenting wine by crushing the local grapes and fermenting the resulting sugars. In the 14th and 15th century the Russians and Scots began distilling vodka and whisky. A Russian Monk inside the Kremlin first produced what we now know as vodka, which he called 'bread wine'. He used a method whereby he would dissolve grain starch, heat and then convert into sugars by adding malt. The end product was very coarse and in some ways had more similarities to whiskey than vodka as it was rough and pungent on the nose. It was not until after the process was refined that it was named 'vodka' after 'voda' the Russian word for water.

In the 16th century, the English began to mass-produce beers and ales. Ale did not contain hops and was darker in colour and fermented in a warmer environment. Beer generally did not contain hops at the time and was fermented in a colder environment, for longer. The Brits often abused alcohol—it was not uncommon for many of the working class men to knock back up to 15–18 pints a day!

By the 17th century, British soldiers were fighting in Holland and took a liking for the locally produced genever (or gin as it became more commonly known). Many of the soldiers used to take a shot (or three) before striding into battle and into enemy fire. This is how the phrase 'Dutch Courage' was coined. The genever of the time was usually a distilled neutral grain spirit mainly flavoured with juniper berries, which were known for their antioxidant qualities and common in Holland.

The popularity of gin accelerated at an alarming pace and by the mid 1750s it was pretty well out of control in the UK with the average consumption being around ¾ a litre per week. The start of London's dry gin production, leading to the prevalence of cheap and inferior gin. This drove the price down to such an extent that it could be bought on the streets of London for as little as one pence per litre, which at the time was cheaper than a loaf of bread. Alcoholism hit such highs (or lows) that it was not unknown for mothers, who had become hooked on the Dutch drop, to give up their newborn baby in return for a tipple of the spirit. At this time it gained another grisly nickname on the streets of London—that of 'mother's ruin'.

'Bathtub Gin' (the name alluded to the fact that it was often homemade and mixed in a bathtub) was now flooding the markets and was readily consumed in Speakeasies. The government tried to quell this thirst for the Dutch liquor by introducing a hefty tax to all makers of gin and the ever-growing mass of distilleries. But, in turn, the country rioted so violently that within a few years the law was repelled.

In the late 1700s, with the advent of the British Navy increasing its global reach, the Navy introduced a rum or gin ration that was administered by the captain of the ship twice daily. This caused problems though, as on many occasions, the sailors would find that in the heat of battle their muskets would jam or not even work at all and cannons misfired, as the gunpowder they were using would often be damp from spilt liquor from rowdy sailors drinking their rations. But rather than removing the alcohol, the Navy decided the only liquor allowed was to be over 100 per cent or 'navy proof', so if it spilt, it would still light. Thus Navy-strength rum and gin were born.

In the 1600s, the British Navy officially introduced rum rations with two 'tots' of navy rum per day for all of the sailors in its fleet. The US Navy introduced a similar but rather more generous 'ration' serving up to half pint of rum per day to their merry sailors!

The alcohol rations became known as 'grog', which came from the Captain who served these rations who often wore a grogram (a coarse fabric coat) or wax-lined jacket to protect him from the elements. The sailors often nicknamed him 'the grog man' and the term stuck to the extent that it is still readily used to this day.

Incredibly enough, these gin and rum rations were not phased out until 1977. In the early 1970s, even the skippers of nuclear submarines were drinking their daily ration of gin or rum while manning these vessels.

Throughout the 1800s, the gin distilleries became licensed and paid controlled taxes accordingly. The thirst for the genever and gin slowed to the extent that it was mainly imbibed in a much more relaxed manner.

Around the mid 1850s the quintessential British tipple the gin and tonic became a popular and altogether more sophisticated way to mix gin. A mix derived from the Chicona Bark (native tree from South America) named quinine was already being ground up and mixed with water in an effort to quell the onset of malaria in the more tropical climes and colonies of the extended British empire. The taste was so vulgar and bitter that many took to covering the bitter taste and potent ordure with a 'healthy' measure of London dry gin—and the 'G and T' was born.

The First Cocktail

By definition a cocktail must be a mix of two or more ingredients. We can categorically trace its first documented mention (and description) back to the *Columbian Repository*, a New York City newspaper in 1806 where it was stated that it was 'a stimulating liquor, composed of spirits of any kind, sugar, water and bitters it is vulgarly called a bittered sling'. But we know for sure that they were around way before this, even if in a basic and crude form.

Around the period of the 14 and 15th century some of the first cocktails were being mixed, albeit without a great deal of skill and precision. It became quite common practice for many seafarers, sailors and even pirates of the time to save up their daily ration of rum or gin to mix with any ingredient that they might find on their travels. More often than not it was sugarcane, sugar, mint and citrus fruit to make the drink more palatable. This made the cheap rum a more palatable finish, as well as softening the harshness of the crude rum.

With the poor diets and over-indulgence of liquor on board the ships of the time, it's hardly surprising they had many issues with ill health and in particular scurvy, which is caused by a deficiency of vitamin C. In the early 1700s, doctors travelling on these ships would often prescribe fresh lime to be drunk with their gin rations. Lime juice was especially high in vitamin C so would help relieve the symptoms of scurvy. The sailors would often just mix the juiced limes with gin. This crude cocktail of sorts was named after Mr John T Gimlet, a captain of one of these ships—the Gimlet. And the British sailors were nicknamed 'Limeys' by their American counterparts as many chewed limes throughout the day.

In later years, the fresh limes were to be replaced with cordial as it was easier to store and would not waste as quickly as fresh limes. The Gimlet went on to become one of the world's great cocktails, and is still consumed en masse to this day.

In the early part of the 1800s, New Orleans was becoming a leading player in a slowly emerging 'cocktail culture' with absinthe. Absinthe was traditionally produced from a neutral grain spirit flavoured with wormwood, green anise (from which it gains its green hue) and sweet fennel.

It originated in Switzerland but was readily drunk by the French, who took this indulgence of absinthe with them when settling in the Deep South of the United States. Over time, it became the Americans who would often head down to the French Quarter (Southeast New Orleans) of the city for their fix of absinthe. It was often served neat, with sugar and water and then flamed in the glass.

Often, it would be served in a small eggcup-type glass (as originally used by the French in their homeland), named a 'coquetier'. Many historians believe that it actually might have been at this time that the word 'cocktail' became commonplace as it was thought many Americans would head to the French Quarter and ask for a cocktail as they would mistakenly mispronounce the word 'coquetier'!

There was also another basic mixed cocktail known as the Sazerac that was starting to become popular around the mid-1800s in New Orleans, named after the French cognac Sazerac de Forge, this cognac was stirred with Sugar Peychard Bitters (a pharmaceutical bitters) and chilled water.

There are also records of the first Manhattan cocktail around this period, although it did not become popular until the late 1800s when it was recreated for Lady Jenny Churchill (Winston Churchill's mother) at the Manhattan Club—more than likely where the drink gained its name—in New York City. The history of this drink is a little grey. However, what we are absolutely sure about is that in 1830 Jeremiah Thomas was born in Sackets Harbour NYC. He would move to New York City in the mid 1800s and open his first Salon Bar and go on to write the world's first cocktail book *The Bartender's Guide: How To Mix Drinks*. This was a historic moment in cocktail culture as this gave documented and measured listings of many cocktails; bartenders in the US then eventually around the globe finally had some standard recipes to follow.

Listed in this book were some of the benchmarks for mixed drinks creations. Drinks such as Flips, Fizzes, Sours and Punch became globally recognised and gave bartenders many base formulas to work from and allowed them to create their own variations. Still to this day these drinks recipes are an important part of any bartender's repertoire.

'Professor' Jerry Thomas, as he was often known (this nickname relating to his professionalism and showmanship rather than any academic scholarship), took his bartending show on the road around the US and later Europe. He really was the world's first professional bartender and would entertain the punters with flair. He was paid over $100 USD per week, which was, in those days, more than the Vice President of the United States!

The 'Professor' passed away in the late 1800s leaving an immense legacy behind. His impact on global cocktail culture was unparalleled and his books are still a key point of reference today for many bartenders. In memory of his work, in 2004 a cocktail museum was opened in New Orleans, founded by Dale De Groff and Chris McMillan. It is an amazing tribute to all things 'cocktail' and features a life-size model of the 'Professor'.

In the early part of the 20th century, just before the prohibition laws came into effect in the United States, several other all-time classics were created—the Cuba Libre in the early 1900s, (Cuba) and the Daiquiri (also Cuba) and evidence also of the first Dry Martini being mixed in 1910 (New York).

As a side note, the Martini was famously the go-to drink of none other than the one and only Mr James Bond. However, in the novels written by Ian Fleming, this was not his first choice of tipple. Preferring neat scotch, Pol Roger champagne and the odd Negroni or three. Fleming himself worked for MI5 and many of his experiences and drinking habits were built into the novels. He became so fond of one drink in particular, the Vesper Martini, that he made it Bond's drink of choice in Casino Royale mixed to his very own specifications.

Prohibition!

On 29 January 1920, prohibition of alcohol in the US was announced, and it would change the face of cocktail history.

The act would not only fuel the public's demand for alcohol, but it would also create 'the speakeasy'—illegal bars and taverns. All prohibition really did was to increase the crime rate immensely as well as the bootlegging of illegal liquor.

Speakeasies exploded across the country—New York was home to over 100,000 of these and Chicago almost 10,000. These speakeasies would often be housed under trapdoors, false floors or behind secret panels in bookcases mainly to avoid detection from the many police raids that would take place.

In these secret venues it was encouraged to 'speakeasy' to avoid detection thus creating the nickname used for these illicit drinking taverns.

Some of these bars have been meticulously restored, especially in New York. Bars such as PDT, Angels Share and Employees Only are fantastic modern twists on the original illegal drinking parlour.

PDT (Please Don't Tell) is a 'must visit' if you are ever bar crawling in the Big Apple. You enter through a regular-looking NYC hot dog stand then enter a phone booth, head along a secret passage until you reach the inside of a very cool classic Irish-style bar from the 1920s welcomes you, complete with taxidermy.

The onset of prohibition not only severely increased the general crime rate but also increased the presence of the Mafia (especially in NYC and Chicago) who quickly found that there were some rather large business opportunities in both the creation and selling of bootleg liquor. Probably the most well-known of these Mafia gangsters was the legendary Al Capone who was known to own over half of Chicago's speakeasies as well as being involved in prostitution and dodgy deeds in the 1920s and 30s.

The law eventually caught up with Capone who was sent to the infamous high security prison island of Alcatraz in San Francisco Bay for tax invasion. However, this was not before amassing an incredible 70 million USD (about 1.5 billion USD in today's money) from his various businesses. Capone was released in 1939 and died in 1947, just before his 50th birthday, of a heart attack.

The production of bootleg liquor during this period of prohibition even outside of the mafia was also booming. Many people would produce their own whiskey often with the risk of major health risks or even death, as it was dangerously impure. A medicinal tonic that was distilled with Jamaican ginger extract, with an alcohol content of nearly 70 per cent, which was nicknamed 'Jake' was known to cause paralysis as it contained an unhealthy level of tricresyl phosphate (TCP). TCP was initially added to water down the alcohol but the manufacturers at the time did not realise that it was also highly toxic.

This style of liquor became so popular that many of the people who'd indulged could be spotted by the paralysis in their limbs, often dragging their leg or dropping an arm by their side!

Doctors would prescribe alcohol illegally on the black market for ill health and in turn visits to the doctor became ever more popular and doctors were becoming increasingly corrupt in return for a prescription of the right 'tonic'.

Liquor was being produced in homemade stills and served in teacups and jam jars to avoid detection while consuming. Cocktail creation during this period also reached a creative high—although certainly not in the US.

Due to the lack of jobs in the US, many bartenders left the country to ply their trade overseas, in countries such as the UK, France and Cuba, which were free of prohibition. This created amazing bars such as Harry's New York Bar in Paris and Harry's Bar in Venice.

In Harry's Bar, Paris, which was opened by a bartender from New York called Harry Mcelhone. All-time classic cocktails, such as the Bloody Mary, the Sidecar, the White Lady and the Blue Lagoon were created, mixed and shaken there.

The original Bloody Mary was created as a morning 'pick-me-up' as it was thought that the vitamin D and iron in the tomato juice would clear the worst of a hangover and if it didn't the double shot of vodka certainly would!

In Harry's Bar in Venice, the Champagne Bellini was first mixed by Giuseppe Cipriani.

In Cuba, bars such as El Floridita, La Bodeguita del Medio and Sloppy Joe's were often manned by travelling American bartenders and became hip hangouts for celebrities such as Frank Sinatra, John Wayne and Clark Gable. Drinks such as the Daiquiri and Mojito were said to have been created or popularised during this period of prohibition in the United States.

Classic Cocktails, 1880–1930

Gimlet

(Modern Recipe)

70 ml/2⅖ fl oz gin or vodka
10 ml/⅓ fl oz lime cordial (roses)

Stir and strain into a chilled martini glass. Garnish with a lemon or lime twist.

Created pretty well by accident when the British Navy began mixing gin rations with fresh lime in a bid to prevent scurvy on the ships.

Circa 1750

Sazerac

(Modern Recipe)

60 ml/2 fl oz rye whiskey
10 ml/⅓ fl oz absinthe (Parisian)
dash of Peychard Bitters
dash of sugar syrup

Fill glass with crushed ice and pour absinthe over ice then pour rest of ingredients into mixing glass and stir then empty crushed ice and strain into glass.

Garnish with a lemon twist and discard or drop into a glass.

A deep south classic first created to sell Antoine Peychard's 'Peychard Bitters' and made in his pharmacy in New Orleans.

Circa 1800

Dry Martini

(Modern Recipe)

70 ml/2½ fl oz gin or vodka
10 ml/⅓ fl oz Noilly Prat vermouth

Stir and strain into a chilled martini glass. Garnish with a lemon twist or an olive. Wash with vermouth and then discard.

Early documentation can trace the martini back to the mid to late 1800s but there is documented proof this style of dry martini was created by Martini di Arma di Taggia in the early 1900s at The Knickerbocker Hotel, NYC.

Circa 1910

Manhattan

(Perfect)

50 ml/1¾ fl oz bourbon
10 ml/⅓ fl oz sweet vermouth
10 ml/⅓ fl oz dry vermouth
dash of bitters
dash of cherry juice

Stir and strain into a chilled martini glass. Garnish with a lemon twist and cherry.

Circa mid-1800s

Gibson

70 ml/2 ½ fl oz gin
10 ml/⅓ fl oz dry vermouth

Stir all ingredients over ice and strain into chilled martini glass.

Created for artist Charles Dana Gibson by bartender Charlie Connolly at NYC Players Club.

Circa 1900

James Bond Cocktail

50 ml/1¾ fl oz vodka
1 sugar cube, soaked in angostura bitters
top with champagne

Build and stir into a champagne flute.

Created by a bartender at Harry's New York Bar in Paris for James Bond author Ian Fleming.

Circa 1920

Alfonso

1 sugar cube, soaked in angostura bitters
20 ml/⅔ fl oz Dubonet
top with champagne

Place sugar cube into a champange glass. Pour in rest of ingredients. Garnish with a lemon twist.

Named after the Spanish King Alfonso XIII

Circa 1936

Cuba Libre

50 ml/1¾ fl oz light rum
cola
lime squeeze, to garnish

Add rum then top with cola. Garnish with a lime squeeze.

Created during the revolutionary war in Cuba when light rum was mixed with Coca Cola and named 'Cuba Libre' or 'Free Cuba' by the soldiers.

Circa 1901

Daiquiri

(modern/revised)

60 ml/2 fl oz light rum
20 ml/⅔ fl oz fresh squeezed fresh lime juice
10 ml/⅓ fl oz sugar syrup

Shake and strain into a chilled martini glass. Garnish with a twist of lime or lime wheel.

Original recipe can be traced back to the Daiquiri mines in Cuba and a gentleman by the name of Jennings Cox who created this drink when he ran out of gin.

Circa 1905

Singapore Sling
(original)

40 ml/1½ fl oz gin
60 ml/2 fl oz cherry liqueur (or cherry brandy)
5 ml/⅕ fl oz cointreau
5 ml/⅕ fl oz DOM Bénédictine
10 ml/⅓ fl oz grenadine
80 ml/2½ fl oz pineapple juice
30 ml/1 fl oz fresh lemon juice
1 dash Angostura bitters

Shake and strain into a highball glass. Serve long over ice with a garnish of orange slice and cherry.

One of the world's most recognisable cocktails from Raffles Hotel by Ngiam Tong Boon.

Circa 1915

Death in the Afternoon

(modern recipe)

20 ml/⅔ fl oz absinthe (Parisian)
dash of sugar
dash of lemon juice
top with champagne

Build into a chilled champagne glass and garnish with a twist of lemon.

Sometimes known as the Hemingway Champagne Cocktail, said to be created by American author and cocktail afficianado, Mr Ernest Hemingway himself, although the original had a staggering 50 ml/1¾ fl oz of absinthe! Named after his 1932 book *Death in the Afternoon* about Spanish bullfighting.

Circa 1935

The Martinez
(modern version)

60 ml/2 fl oz gin
15 ml/½ fl oz sweet vermouth
15 ml/½ fl oz dry vermouth
5 ml/⅕ fl oz maraschino liqueur
1 dash angostura bitters

Stir and strain into a vintage martini coupet. Garnish with an orange zested twist.

Original recipes can be found in an early Jerry Thomas recipe, which can be traced to the late 1800s and created with Genever Gin.

Circa 1870 (original)

The Bronx

50 ml/1¾ fl oz London dry gin
15 ml/½ fl oz sweet vermouth
15 ml/½ fl oz dry vermouth
15 ml/½ fl oz fresh squeezed orange juice

Shake and strain into a chilled martini glass and orange twist garnish.

Created by Johnny Solon in NYC and named after the Bronx Zoo where he once went after consuming a fair few of these and thought he saw many strange and wonderful animals.

Circa 1907

The Algonquin

50 ml/1¾ fl oz rye
15 ml/½ fl oz dry martini
20 ml/⅔ fl oz pineapple juice

Shake and strain into a chilled martini glass.

First created at the Algonquin Hotel in NYC.

Circa 1930

Bamboo

30 ml/1 fl oz dry sherry
30 ml/1 oz sweet vermouth
dash of orange bitters

Stir and strain into a chilled martini.

Derived from Harry Craddock's *Savoy Cocktail Book* 1930.

Circa 1930

Blue Lagoon

50 ml/1¾ fl oz vodka
20 ml/⅔ fl oz blue curacao
120 ml/4 fl oz pineapple juice

Shake and strain into a long or hurricane glass and garnish with a lemon slice.

Difficult to substantiate although Harry's New York Bar Paris lays claim.

Circa 1980

Trilby Cocktail

70 ml/2 ½ fl oz dry vermouth
dash of Cointreau
dash of Peychard
10 ml/⅓ fl oz bourbon float

Stir first 3 ingredients and strain into a coupet glass and then float whiskey and garnish with lemon twist.

Creator unknown.

Circa 1900

Old-Fashioned
(Modern Recipe)

70 ml/2⅖ fl oz bourbon
3–4 dashes of cherry juice
3–4 dashes of orange bitters
dash sugar

Build and stir and add chipped ice. Garnish with 2 orange twists.

One of the world's first popular cocktails and can be traced back to the early 1800s and possibly the drink of mention in 1806 NYC newspaper *The Balance and Columbian Repository.*

Circa 1805

London Fog

60 ml/2 fl oz gin
15 ml/½ fl oz absinthe

Shake and strain into a wine glass full of crushed ice.

Created in the 1950s by a London bartender and named after London's infamous 'fog', which was in fact pollution.

Circa 1940

Bloody Mary
(original Pete Petiot recipe 1920)

a very large measure of vodka
15 ml/½ fl oz lemon juice
black pepper and salt
3 dashes Worcestershire
2 drops Tabasco sauce

Build into a highball glass. Garnish with a lemon wedge.

Created by Fenand 'Pete' Petiot. One story for the name of the cocktail was he named it after a barmaid, Mary, who worked at a New York Bar named The Bucket Of Blood.

Circa 1920s

Sidecar

50 ml/1¾ fl oz cognac
25 ml/¾ fl oz cointreau
15 ml/½ fl oz lemon juice
dash of sugar syrup or water (optional)

Shake and strain into a vintage glass. Garnish with a twist of lemon.

Harry's New York Bar, Paris created by Harry Macelhone for an American Army Captain when suffering a cold. After indulging in a few he was known to have to take a sidecar home.

Circa 1920s

Ping Pong

50 ml/1¾ fl oz sloe gin
10 ml/⅓ fl oz fresh lemon juice
10ml/⅓ fl oz egg white

Shake and strain into a vintage glass.

There are early traces of this recipe as far back as 1902/03 in the bartenders encyclopaedia, made with scotch or bourbon. But this more modern interpretation is from the 1920s in San Francisco when Sloe Gin was preferred and, not particularly potent, was seen as the perfect mid ping pong game tipple as not too strong to put you off your game!

Circa 1927

The Twentieth Century Cocktail

50 ml/1¾ fl oz gin
25 ml/¾ fl oz Lillet Blanc
25 ml/¾ fl oz white cacao
25 ml/¾ fl oz fresh lemon juice
dash sugar

Shake and strain into a cocktail glass and garnish with a lemon twist and grated dark chocolate.

Created at Café Royal, London and named after a famous locomotive that ran between New York and Chicago.

Circa 1937

Charlie Chaplin

30 ml/1 fl oz sloe gin
30 ml/1 fl oz apricot brandy
30 ml/1 fl oz fresh lime juice
dash egg white (optional)

Shake well and strain into a chilled vintage glass.

Garnish with a lime twist.

Originated in the "Old Waldorf Bar Days" cocktail book. The Waldorf Astoria in New York created this in honor of the one and only Sir Charles Chaplin.

Circa 1910–1920

White Lady

50 ml/1¾ fl oz gin
25 ml/¾ fl oz cointreau
15 ml/½ fl oz lemon juice
1 egg white

Shake and strain into a vintage glass. Garnish with a lemon twist.

Yet another Harrys New York Bar classic and possibly a twist on an earlier drink made with Cointreau brandy and crème de menthe.

Circa 1929

Prohibition Iced Tea

15 ml/½ fl oz vodka
15 ml/½ fl oz light rum
15 ml/½ fl oz absinthe
15 ml/½ fl oz gin
30 ml/1 fl oz lemon juice
10 ml/⅓ fl oz sugar syrup

Shake and strain into a tin and garnish with a lime squeeze.

A twist on the Long Island iced tea, possibly created to disguise the imbibing of alcohol during US prohibition.

Circa 1920-1930

CHAPTER TWO
Classics & Twists

Classics & Twists

Contemporary cocktails can be categorised as drinks created post-prohibition and into the 'Jazz era' from the early 1930s through to the late 1960s and 70s. As with the pre-prohibition and prohibition era, this period also produced many of the all-time great cocktails many of which are still found in great bars around the world.

Tiki Culture

Many bars in the 1930s and 40s were still selling classic cocktails from prohibition times. Although these drinks were originally created and consumed behind closed doors, the Jazz era popularised them. Hollywood icons (and cocktail appreciators) such as Clark Gable, Katherine Hepburn and Humphrey Bogart brought their own brand of silver screen romance and cool to these drinks and, in turn, brought cocktail culture into the mainstream.

In the mid-1930s a young man Victor Bergran, or 'Trader Vic' as he was more commonly known, opened a small restaurant in Oakland, California named Hinky Dinks, which would later be known as Trader Vic's. This was the first themed bar/restaurant of any kind in the mainland USA. Trader Vic's was decorated with wooden carved Tiki's, fishing nets, old lanterns, themed and odd shaped glassware and old framed pictures mostly with a nautical theme. The success of these restaurants marked the end of the oppressed drinking parlours of the prohibition era and the beginning of a new wave of casual venues that became prolific in the '30s.

Trader Vic was known to have created such Tiki classics as the Zombie, Three Dots and A Dash and the Navy Grog, all extremely very fine drinks which stand up well even in today's more refined cocktail culture. Even though these drinks were quite heavy on the liquor they were so well balanced that they were still easy on the palate. For example, Three Dots and a Dash has a mix of three different rums (one being overproof) but the blend of these rums was softened with fresh pressed orange juice, honey water and spice syrup. These ingredients help to balance the drink to perfection and if there was ever a key to a great and well-made drink it is balance—never too strong or weak and never too sour or too sweet. Many of the best drinks in the Tiki style use the old Caribbean methodology of mixing drinks using the rhyme: *One of sour, two of sweet, three of strong, four of weak.* Based on the three dots and a dash the recipe would be as follows:

1 part lime
½ part each honey water and spice syrup
3 parts strong (3 rums)
4 parts weak (the fresh-pressed orange juice)

Trader Vic also franchised his restaurants around the world with one of the most popular in Waikiki, Hawaii—at its peak there were 25 restaurants in the city alone. But it was in Hawaii where the name 'Tiki' was cemented as the name of these Polynesian-style drinks. Many US soldiers returned from Hawaii to the mainland after the war, speaking highly about this style of Tiki restaurant/bar and the appetite of the Americans was duly charged.

Mostly the soldiers enjoyed the total escapism of the whole concept both with the venue theme and fun (and very strong) drinks. Customers were often encouraged to let off some steam. Impromptu sing-a-longs and drinking competitions were also commonplace. Many of the soldiers felt that they could, at least for a while, forget about the war in these bars and they held fond memories for them upon returning home.

The word tiki was derived from a Hawaiian God or 'tiki' and many of the mugs that these drinks were served in were in the shape of these Hawaiian Gods. I personally love the kitsch and fun tiki-style drinks and the whole scene around them. Drinks served in flaming skulls and volcano bowls and in a variety of glassware and ceramics. It's a frivolous and celebratory drinking culture that also reflected the history of the tropics and Polynesia in a very tongue-in-cheek manner. These bars laid the foundations for a flood of chain and themed restaurants over the next 40–50 years such TGI Fridays, Planet Hollywood and Denny's. Unfortunately now, many of the best Tiki bars are to be found outside of the US (and Hawaii) with Trailer Happiness in London and Hula Bula in Perth being two great examples.

On the island of Oahu there is really only one remaining authentic tiki bar left standing. It's called La Mariana on the shore of the Keehi Lagoon, Honolulu. This was opened in 1957 during the hey day of tiki drinks and pays homage to 1950s Hawaiian décor and tiki themes with relics from many of the old tiki bars that have now closed their doors on the island, such as Trader Vics and The Tahitian Lenai. In turn it has become a bit of a tiki geek hang out with people travelling from afar to enjoy the drinks and atmosphere.

Margarita Madness

While tiki culture was booming on the west coast of the USA, in the south at around the same time the Margarita was born. There are a few varied stories as to its original creation but one that has more than a touch of romance is that of a head barkeep from Galveston, Texas. He created a drink for the love of his life, a singer named Peggy Lee (her name equates to Margarita in Spanish). He knew she liked tequila so made it with a base of tequila. When he first set eyes on her she was wearing a green dress so he laced the drink with lime juice to represent this image he carried in his mind. He then added triple sec to balance the drink and then garnished the drink with a salt rim as he thought of her as an angel and this represented her halo. This creation went on to become an all-time contemporary classic and drew many who did not even really enjoy tequila into savoring this drink.

If you ever head to the tequila country of Mexico, be sure to get out of the cities and visit some of the amazing tequila distilleries in the lowlands and highlands to the east of Guadalajara. This region is home to the Blue Agave plant from which tequila is derived. The general rule that is that tequila from the highlands is slightly sweeter than the tequila in the lowlands of Mexico due to the different soils in which the plant is grown. It is slightly wetter and cooler in the highlands thus producing a different soil type that produces a sweeter agave. In the lowlands, however, the dryer and warmer conditions produce a more earthy agave and very much less sweet, as with wine.

A visit to a distillery can often end in a boisterous night out drinking tequila shots and margarita's, and dancing in a Hacienda, which is testament to the unwavering hospitality of the Mexican people. Although it is always best to exercise caution (especially after a few drops of the agave nectar) as many cities close to the distilleries have high crime rates.

Vodka

While tequila was gaining popularity in Mexico in the 1940s and '50s, another, quite different, spirit was gaining momentum on the other side of the world. Vodka had been rather heavily consumed in Eastern Europe, but it was never drunk elsewhere and definitely did not feature in any cocktails from the previously mentioned eras. This was to change rather rapidly with the creation of a vodka-based cocktail that came to be known as the Moscow Mule, in the early 1940s.

A gentleman by the name of John Martin discovered a vodka named Smirnoff, from Russia. He decided that this might well be 'the next big thing' in the United States and invested heavily in importing a huge number of pallets of the Russian spirit into the USA. The only problem was convincing the hardened local drinking population of Los Angeles that they should jump ship from their usual tipple of American whiskey, rum and gin to vodka. This was a tough task, as the rather harsh liquor did not become the overnight success Mr Graham was hoping for. So he was stuck with a vast amount of vodka just sitting on the docks.

One night he was drowning his sorrows in a bar named The Cock and Bull on the Sunset Strip in downtown LA when he met the owner Jack Morgan, who was also having a few liveners. Morgan was also down on his luck having produced a large amount of his new spicy ginger beer but could not sell it.

So over a few too many drinks they decided to join forces, cut their loses and combine the ginger beer with the vodka and serve in a tin mug—purely for novelty value. The production of this drink was made easier by the close proximity of a nearby copper mill. And so the Moscow Mule was born, its name derived from the fact that Smirnoff was from Moscow and, combined with the ginger, it had a kick like a mule as often a double or triple shot of vodka was used. A mule went on to become the emblem embossed on the copper mug.

The polaroid camera had just been invented so Martin decided to travel around the country, asking bartenders to pose with their Moscow Mules. These photos would then be passed around to other bars to show what they were missing out on. The Moscow Mule was really the world's first strategically marketed drink.

Soon the drink and the consumption of vodka, spread like wildfire across the country and a vodka cocktail culture was born. Sales of vodka increased ten-fold in the US within five years and the Moscow Mule reached legendary status just as quickly. It was the hip drink of the Hollywood set with stars such Woody Allen and Sammy Davis Jnr having their own inscribed copper mug behind the bar at The Cock and Bull.

Meanwhile, over in the UK, Winston Churchill also had a taste for hard liquor, French champagne and the odd cocktail or three. His daily routine was well documented and was namely scotch (early/mid morning) Pol Roger champagne, (lunchtime) followed by rounds of scotch and the odd martini (dinner).

Churchill's fondness for the hard stuff didn't tarnish his popularity and, in fact, he was a kind of cocktail and liquor ambassador for the ages. He was well renowned for never getting intoxicated even with his huge intake of alcohol.

In 1955 just at the end of Churchill's rein as British PM, a young group of entertainers, including Sammy Davis Jnr, Frank Sinatra and Dean Martin, would become known as 'the Rat Pack' and became some of the most well-known entertainers on the planet. But they would become equally as famous for their womanising and hard liquor drinking sessions as for their acting and singing careers.

Creative Cocktails

The decades of the 1960s and 1970s brought in a new era that was less about glamour and Hollywood stars and more about disco and recreational drugs—neither of which were conducive to the creation or consumption of cocktails.

In the 1990s, the cocktail was back with a vengeance, with the dynamic cocktail scenes of New York and London leading the charge. Bars in London such as Dicks Bar at The Atlantic, The Lab and Quaglinos led the way in the cool category. While TGI Fridays in Covent Garden also became a cocktail mecca, selling around 10,000 cocktails a week. While New York's meatpacking district was being transformed into a vibrant, hip eating, drinking and clubbing hangout, which epitomised the changes happening with food and beverage within the city. The mid 1990s also saw Ian Schrager and W Hotels revolutionise the boutique hotel and hotel lobby bar scene with first Morgans Hotel on Madison Avenue then The Hudson on West 58th Street, New York, followed by the first W HOTEL on Lexington Avenue.

The creations were more sophisticated with many bars insisting on using not only the highest quality ingredients but the best quality liquor available. Vintage champagne sales spiked in these new bars as did bottle service and the consumption of luxury spirits such a Grey Goose, Belvedere and Patron Tequila.

Bartenders became more creative as Dick Bradsel in London and his New York counterpart, Dale De Groff, took classic cocktails and put approachable and modern twists on them. Classic cocktails from the 20s, 30s and 40s came back to life especially in De Groff's famous reincarnation—the Cosmopolitan. This had a direct impact on the revival of the classic cocktail in the early and mid-2000s.

The inventiveness of some leading chefs in the early 1990s such as Ferran Adria at El Bulli, had a direct impact on drink making in the early 2000s. People like Tony Canigliaro (from 69 Colebrooke Road, London) used many of these techniques to transform the art of drink-making and signalled the next big step in cocktail culture.

Mojito

(modern recipe)

45 ml/1½ fl oz white rum
3–4 lime squeeze
6–8 mint leaves
10 ml/⅓ fl oz lemon juice
soda

Build and stir into a highball. Fill with crushed ice and top up with soda. Garnish with a mint sprig.

Derived from the Cuban word 'Mojo' meaning 'soul'.

Circa 1920s (popularised)

Margarita
(Danny Negrete, 1936)

40 ml/1½ fl oz Gold Tequila
40 ml/1½ fl oz triple sec
40 ml/1½ fl oz tequila
squeezed lime

Shake and strain. Serve in a martini glass. Garnish with a lime twist.

Danny Negrete created a similar recipe in Mexico in 1936 and served it with crushed ice.

Circa 1936

Between the Sheets

30 ml/1 fl oz white rum
30 ml/1 fl oz Cointreau
15 ml/½ fl oz lemon juice
30 ml/1 fl oz cognac

Shake and strain into a chilled martini glass.

Variation on the classic Sidecar. First appeared at Harrys New York Bar.

Circa 1930s

Aviation

60 ml/2 fl oz London Dry Gin
15 ml/½ fl oz lemon juice
15 ml/½ fl oz maraschino
10 ml/⅓ fl oz crème de violette

Shake and strain. Serve in a vintage coupette. Garnish with a cherry.

Harry Craddock Savoy Cocktail Book.

Circa 1930s

The Vesper Martini
(1950s)

60 ml/2 fl oz Boodles Gin
30 ml/1 fl oz Russian vodka
15 ml/½ fl oz Kina Lillet (Lillet Blanc)

Shake and strain. Serve with a lemon twist.

Created for Ian Fleming by a bartender at Dukes Bar in London.

Circa 1952

Black (and White) Russian

45 ml/1½ fl oz vodka
20 ml/⅔ fl oz Kahlua

Stir and pour over chipped ice.

For White Russian add:
30 ml/1 fl oz cream

Build and stir.

Originated at the Metropole Hotel, Brussels.

Circa 1949, White Russian 1960s

Zombie

(original recipe)

15 ml/½ fl oz white rum
30 ml/1 fl oz golden rum
30 ml/1 fl oz dark rum
15 ml/½ fl oz 151-proof rum
30 ml/1 fl oz lime juice
1 teaspoon pineapple juice
1 teaspoon papaya juice
1 teaspoon sugar

Blend and serve in a tall glass. Garnish with a mint sprig.

History: Donn Beech at The Beachcombers, LA.

Circa 1940

Pina Colada

45 ml/1½ fl oz light rum
25 ml/¾ fl oz Coco Lopez (coconut cream)
15 ml/½ fl oz crème de coconut
80 ml/2½ fl oz pineapple juice
dash of sugar syrup

Blend with crushed ice until smooth. Serve in a tall glass with a pineapple and cherry garnish.

Created at the Caribe Hilton, Puerto Rico by Ramon Marrero

Circa 1954

Cosmopolitan
(modern Grant Collins recipe)

50 ml/1¾ fl oz Belvedere Citrus Vodka
15 ml/½ fl oz Cointreau
40 ml/1½ fl oz cranberry juice
10 ml/⅓ fl oz lemon juice
dash of sugar

Shake well into a chilled martini glass and garnish with an orange twist.

Original recipes can be traced back to 1970 but has evolved repeatedly over the years.

Circa 1970–2005

Bellini

50 ml/1¾ fl oz white peach puree
top with Prosecco

Serve in a champagne flute and stir.

Created by Giuseppe Cipriani named after Italian Artist Giovanni Bellini.

Circa 1938–40

Planters Punch

50 ml/1¾ fl oz dark rum
20 ml/⅔ fl oz light rum
30 ml/1 fl oz orange juice
dash grenadine

Shake and strain over ice into a highball. Garnish with an orange twist.

Donn Beech discovered this drink and ensured it was one of the first drinks on the list when he opened Don The Beachcombers in California. This is just one of several recipes from the list.

Circa 1934

El Diablo

50 ml/1¾ fl oz tequila
15 ml/½ fl oz crème de cassis
Top with ginger beer.

Serve in a highball glass over ice and garnish with a lime squeeze.

Meaning 'the devil' in Spanish. History and creator unclear.

Circa 1947

Caipiroska

60 ml/2 fl oz vodka
1 whole lime, quartered
2 teaspoons fine sugar

Muddle all and stir in an old-fashioned glass. Then add crushed ice and stir.
Garnish with a lime slice.

As vodka became more popular in the 1970s and 1980s the Caipirinha (same drink with South American rum) started getting changed with vodka—this was the result.

Popularised 1970/80s

Moscow Mule

50 ml/1¾ fl oz Russian vodka
Top with homemade ginger beer

Build over ice and garnish with 2 lime squeezes. Serve in a copper mug.

Originally created at The Cock 'n' Bull in Los Angeles
by Jack Morgan and John Graham.

Circa 1940s

Long Island Iced Tea
(Robert Butt recipe)

2 cups ice cubes
1 part vodka
1 part gin
1 part white rum
1 part white tequila
½ part triple sec
½ part sour mix
1 splash cola
lemon wedges, for garnish

Shake and strain well into a highball glass with ice. Garnish with a lemon squeeze.

Many people seem to think that this drink was created during prohibition, as it looked more like an iced tea than a cocktail in an era when it was vital to ensure any beverage did not resemble anything alcoholic. But I tend to lean towards believing that it was a good few years after this by a gentleman named Robert Butt at the Oak Beach Inn, Long Island, USA. Either way it is a modern-day classic.

Circa 1972

Harvey Wallbanger

45 ml/1 ½ fl oz vodka
fill with orange juice
top with Galliano

Build over ice into a highball glass.
Garnish with an orange slice and a cherry.

Created by Duke Anton and is basically a Screwdriver (vodka and orange) with a top of Galliano. Possibly named after a surfer named Harvey who crashed out of a surfing competition in Newport California and over indulged on a few of these and walked into a wall ... you can guess the rest!

Circa: 1950

Caipirinha

60 ml/2 fl oz cachaca
1 whole lime, quartered
2 teaspoons fine sugar

Muddle all and stir in an old-fashioned glass. Add crushed ice and stir.
Garnish with a lime squeeze.

Named after the word 'caipira' translated means 'lower class' and was originally a peasants drink as the sugarcane rum Cachaca was the drink of choice for many years. Cachaca first came to light in the 1600s.

Popularised after any date in 1950/1960s

3 Dots and a Dash

30 ml/1 fl oz gold rum
30 ml/1 fl oz dark rum
10 ml/⅓ fl oz OP rum
10 ml/⅓ fl oz lime juice
30 ml/1 fl oz orange juice
15 ml/½ fl oz honey water
15 ml/½ fl oz all-spice syrup
2 dashes angostura

Shake and strain into tiki mug over crushed ice and garnish with 3 cherries and lime wedge.

To make the honey water, mix 300 ml/10½ fl oz honey with 200 ml/7 fl oz water. Simmer for 20 minutes. Add 1 tablespoon sugar. Simmer for further 15 minutes. Add a further 100 ml/3½ fl oz honey and leave to cool.

Morse code for victory and was created by Donn Beach to celebrate the end of World War 2 and welcome home the troops.

Circa Late 1940s

Test Pilot

20 ml/⅔ fl oz light rum
50 ml/1¾ fl oz dark Jamaican rum
10 ml/⅓ fl oz fresh lime juice
15 ml/½ fl oz Falernum
dash Cointreau
dash angostura bitters
dash teaspoon Pernod

Shake and strain into a tiki mug and garnish with a mint sprig.

Donn Beach at Don The Beachcombers.

Popularised 1941

Tequila Sunrise

50 ml/1¾ fl oz tequila
fill with orange juice
float grenadine

Build into a highball and garnish with an orange slice.

An all-time archetypal American classic with a song by The Eagles and a 1980s movie and very synonymous with 1970/80s drinking culture. Creator unknown but we know Gene Sulit was creating them just after prohibition in the 1930s at the Arizona Biltmore in Phoenix, Arizona. Some stories also link it back to a couple of dive bars in L.A.

Popularised 1970s

Mint Julep

90 ml/3 fl oz bourbon
6–8 mint leaves
1 teaspoon sugar

Muddle all in a julep cup add crushed ice. Stir and garnish with a mint sprig.

Recipes can be traced back as far as the mid/late 1800s.

Popularised at The Kentucky Derby in 1938.

Mai Tai

35 ml/1¼ fl oz light rum
15 ml/½ fl oz dark rum
15 ml/½ fl oz orgeat syrup
15 ml/½ fl oz Cointreau
35 ml/1¼ fl oz pineapple juice

Shake and strain into a poco grande glass and garnish with a pineapple slice and cherry.

The name came from 'Mai Tai roa ae' which in Tahitian means 'out of this world' uttered to its creator Victor Bergron at Trader Vic's in San Francisco.

Circa mid-1940s

Zombie

(original 1934 recipe)

50 ml/1¾ fl oz dark rum
50 ml/1¾ fl oz Puerto Rican rum
30 ml/1 fl oz OP Rum
15 ml/½ fl oz Falernum
20 ml/⅔ fl oz freshly squeezed lime juice
10 ml/⅓ fl oz grapefruit juice
dash cinnamon syrup
dash grenadine
dash Pernod/dash bitters

Add ¾ cup crushed ice and blend. Serve in a tall glass and garnish with a mint sprig.

Donn Beach for a guest who did not like flying and so Donn knocked him up one of these after a couple he made the flight but said he felt like a zombie!

Circa late 1930s

Blackbeard's Ghost

40 ml/1½ fl oz dark rum
20 ml/⅔ fl oz apricot brandy
35 ml/1¼ fl oz falernum
25 ml/¾ fl oz lime
2 dashes bitters
20 ml/⅔ fl oz spiced rum float

Shake and strain into a pirate tiki mug.

Garnish with mint, pirate flag, umbrella and red cherry.

Created by Jeff 'Beach bum' Berry and featured in his 1940s book *The Grog Log*.

Circa 1940s

Dr Funk

40 ml/1½ fl oz dark rum
15 ml/½ fl oz grenadine
1 spoon Pernod
top with soda water

Shake and strain into a tiki mug. Garnish with a mint sprig, an orange slice and cherry and and umbrella.

Invented by German-born physician Dr Bernard Funk for his patients in the early 1920s. Popularised by Trader Vic's/Don The Beachcombers in 1940s.

CHAPTER THREE
Progressive & Experimental

Experimental and Progressive Cocktails

In 1988, the term 'molecular and physical gastronomy'—using the appliance of science on food preparation and creation—was coined by a French chemist named Hervé This. He is often referred to as the godfather of molecular gastronomy, as this method is now known. Molecular gastronomy saw equipment such as gastrovacs and rotavapors and elements such as dry ice, liquid nitrogen and nitrous oxide, being used on food for the first time.

Chemistry and Cuisine

In 1996, Ferran Adria started serving some extremely creative amuse-bouches (tidbits) followed by a 16-course degustation in his restaurant El Bulli on the Costa Brava in Spain. While the chef wowed diners with his experimental food, he also started experimenting with liquor, using some progressive culinary techniques and bringing these techniques into the mainstream. So popular was his work that El Bulli was booked three years in advance and many of his techniques, such as deconstruction and turning dining into an 'experience' rather than just heading out to dinner, have been borrowed around the world.

In more recent years, these techniques were progressed by Thomas Keller with his groundbreaking sous vide cooking at the French Laundry in California. Sous vide is a cooking technique by which a piece of produce, such as beef, is placed in a vacuum-sealed bag and cooked in a warm water bath for up to 24 hours. The produce is then finished off on the grill, the idea being that none of the flavour of the meat is lost, keepjng it exceptionally tender and full of its own natural juices.

Heston Blumenthal at the Fat Duck in Bray, UK, is probably best known for bringing liquid nitrogen to the masses, taking many of the techniques Adria had kick-started in Spain and pushing the envelope a little further. He started serving desserts freshly made at the table using liquid nitrogen and began pairing food by its molecular structure rather than by obvious flavour matching. Dishes such as Egg and Bacon Ice Cream and Snail Porridge were created using this technique and refined in his in-house laboratory. Blumenthal pretty well solidified the connection between science and food in a totally and unique way.

This blend of chemistry and cuisine not only made me reconsider the way I structure drinks but also inspired me to research a more scientific approach to creating drinks. I was further intrigued when I saw bartender Wayne Collins demonstrate techniques such as the use of foams and gels to modernise classic cocktails. UK bartender, Tony Canigliaro, was also taking things to another level, applying many Blumenthal techniques to drinks creation while, stateside, Eben Freeman was pushing the boundaries in New York City using similar techniques to Canigliaro, as well as being the first to 'smoke coke'—a technique where he smoked coca cola and mixed it with a heavy rum to create a 'smoked rum and coke'.

Layering

I started experimenting with many of these techniques in 2005. At first some of the techniques were mocked by many in the industry and written off as 'faddish' and 'not real bartending'. Using liquid nitrogen and dry ice as well as deconstructing cocktails at the time was often frowned upon. But as people grew used to this progressive and innovative way of making drinks the trend grew. Bars such as the fantastic Der Raum, Melbourne, and The Tippling Club, Singapore, leading the way in the progressive drinks culture in the southern hemisphere, the trend was also gaining popularity in the US and especially the UK.

Many layers of flavour can be used in progressive drinks-making, with the use of textures, foams, gels, airs and mists. Just by using a simple gelatine foam (hot or cold) or a lecithin emulsion you could put many simple yet remarkable twists on drinks. As well as create new signature drinks and twists on classics.

Creating a foam is as simple as mixing flavoured gelatin into a cream gun then charging it with nitrous oxide and chilling. While an emulsion can use sucrose or lecithin which are emulsifiers, and mixing with say fresh pressed citrus and a little sugar syrup and mixing with a hand blender can create a light citrus foam of tiny bubbles (or emulsion), which can be perfect for drinks such as a Citrus Gimlet. It also works well with food such as a Champagne Emulsion for oysters or even a Guinness one for steak.

Simple classics such as a Martini or Manhattan can be given a modern twist or 'softened' a little for the more modern palate. By using an element already in the drink, such as cherry (Manhattan) or vermouth (Martini), and adding an emulsion of foam onto the surface, the impact of these heavy liquored classics is subdued.

By using dry ice (frozen CO_2), which is -70°C, any liquid could be frozen. With the freezing temperature of liquor being between -18 to -30°C you can make a multitude of cocktails and turn them into sorbets. A frozen Martini or Manhattan sorbet, for example, can be softened by adding a little soda to the mix.

As the cocktail is snap frozen the crystallisation is so fine that the texture is extremely silky smooth—something that is hard to achieve if using a Pacolet or an ice cream maker. Cocktails such as Margaritas, Clover Clubs and Pina Coladas can all be turned into mini sorbets or ice creams served in cones, which adds a new and exciting element to traditional cocktail consumption.

In 2006, after a trip to the US (where I had seen this technique being developed), I got my hands on some liquid nitrogen while working in Sydney (frozen nitrogen-LN2). This stuff is rather more volatile than dry ice as it is -197°C.

Using this liquid under the correct conditions another whole world of cocktail creation became a reality. You can make a flavoured protein-based foam, inject with NO2 canister in a cream gun then portion into a desert spoon and baste in the LN2. This creates a meringue of sorts and bursts upon contact with your mouth while at the same time ejects bellowing dragon like puffs of smoke from your nostrils: a great palate cleanser as well as being simply great theatre. This was something that I had seen being served at the table at The Fat Duck and just thought a parallel technique using cocktails would be fun and different—and it worked well. So well in fact that we ended up throwing Nitro Parties in bars and for launches, with huge queues lining up to sample the frozen cocktails.

In more recent times I have also experimented with flavoured (and alcoholic) caviar, champagne ice poles, edible Long Island Iced Tea (LIIT) marshmallows, cosmopolitan candy floss, bourbon wine gums and chocolates, smoked cocktails, sensory cocktails and washed and baked drinks.

Although not such a glamorous process as the Jekyll and Hyde smoking effect when using LN2 or Dry Ice, 'fat washing' is another technique where you can 'wash' spirits with a fat or flavour, then freeze and fine strain, which just leaves the flavour behind.

This works especially well with dark spirits such as bourbon, rum and even whiskey, as the smokiness from the barrel aging process used in many of these spirits can be drawn out further. By using a smoky bacon, for instance, you can make a Bacon Manhattan (one of the all-time favorites at Zeta, Sydney) or even lamb fat to rinse a light rum and create a 'Sunday Roast Mojito' (Eden Bar, Sydney). Gin can also be used, for instance, and washed with truffle oil for a Truffle Negroni or even Vodka with bacon or spices to add another dimension to your Bloody Mary.

Deconstructing cocktails is another fun way to put a unique take on many well-known drinks. It is also a great way to interact with your guests as these drinks take a little explaining when serving. This is where most of the enjoyment lies for me—watching the guest's face light up as they start to understand the concept or begin to reconstruct the drink. Finding it actually works is very satisfying and not quite as hard as you would think.

This method is also surprisingly educational as it shows guests how a bartender creates drinks using layers of flavour in order to gain the correct and well balanced end product. For example you could deconstruct a Margarita in the following manner.

Deconstructed Margarita

1 chilled water
2 sides of sea salt foam (see recipe below)
3 fresh pieces of lime
4 candied pieces of candied orange slices (see recipe below)
5 slightly sweetened and freshly squeezed lime juice
6 100% agave tequila

Serve on a platter and 'reconstruct' the drinks starting from the last ingredient (six–one above) to the first ingredient taking a sip of each, finishing with the chilled water. The brain takes a while to reshuffle the order of the flavours (normally around 45 seconds to 1 minute) into something it can relate to or reference, as it is not used to receiving flavor data in this broken-up manner.

Sea salt foam
Place 3 sheets of gelatine in 250 ml/9 fl oz of cold water to soften. Combine with 4 tablespoons of sea salt. Bring to the boil then simmer for 25 minutes. Add 45 ml/1½ fl oz sugar. Add water and gelatine to sugar mixture. Using gloves, squeeze the gelatine to dissolve into the mixture. Use a fine strainer to remove excess gelatine. Fill to three-quarters with water, to taste (sweeten as required). Charge with two NO2 bulbs.

Candied orange slices
Soak thinly cut orange slices in Grand Marnier overnight then roll in caster sugar and let sit on some parchment paper in a warm place overnight until crisp.

But as each layer binds to the last it will reconstruct on your palate to become a margarita. To try this experiment again, simply repeat. This above reconstruction works in some ways even better than the original as the salt foam is spooned into your mouth to the area of your palate that receives salty flavours, which is the back of your tongue. Drinking a regular margarita, the salt rim will just hit your lips, an area where you have no specific receptors for this flavour. The result is quite impressive as it actually makes you salivate and increases the enjoyment of your deconstruction because salivating causes the gastric juices in your stomach to flow as your body expects food.

Sensory Engagement

The technique of engaging different senses while has been used by progressive chefs such as Adria and Blumenthal for sometime. Inspired by this use of 'sensory engagement' I experimented with many different drinks and possibilities. The first of which was a range of sensory drinks such as a 'Sensory Colada' or a 'Sensory Martini' and was covered by *The New York Times*. For the colada I would first give the guest a lei and place around their neck, just to get them in the mood (sight). I would serve the colada in a pineapple (sight/touch) then blindfold the guest. Next I would play some tropical tiki beats (sound) and spray a coconut mist in front of them that smelt like the tropics (smell) and would be sprayed intermittently each minute. Finally, I would place a small fan and a heat lamp in front of them (at a safe distance) to finish of the experience. The idea behind doing these things is so that the drinker is transported to a tropical beach with the music, smell of the beach, heat and soft sea breeze while sipping a colada (taste). While with the martini you would be instantly whisked off to a NY dive bar circa 1940s. As we played you tunes by Sinatra, Tony Bennett and Sammy Davis Jnr. Blindfolded you would be sprayed a light cigar smoke mist in front of you. So popular were these new techniques that we sold them by the dozen when we did promotions in various bars.

In the last few years, many bartenders have been pushing the envelope further by using tinctures (flavoured alcohol-based essences) made using a rotavapor and a chemist's still.

A rotavapor is a piece of chemistry apparatus that is more likely to be found in a lab than in a cocktail bar or kitchen. Its regular use is to remove solvents from liquid samples by evaporation. All different substances have various boiling points and the levels at which they evaporate differ. So if you know the temperature that some specific liquid evaporates then you can draw it out off the sample. How does this work in a bar I might hear you ask?

The short answer is it simply does not. But it can be used for varied preparation. For instance, it is great for extracting essential oils out of pretty well anything. So you might want to extract the lemon and lime extract from the fruit. Place the skins into 100% pure alcohol (ethanol) and let sit for 24 hours, strain then place into the rotavapor. The glass bulb of the rotavapor revolves as it sits in a water bath and slowly heats. Eventually the ethanol will evaporate first (as it has the lower boiling point), leaving behind the essential oils. Mix this oil with alcohol to make an alcoholic extract or 'tincture'. Alcoholic flavors can be made from pretty well any solid, plant or herb. I have seen guys go to the extreme of taking flavour extracts from slate, granite and even grape seeds to impart unusual flavours into their drinks.

Another tool used to deconstruct cocktails is a gastrovac. This item is basically a vacuum pump with a chamber. It withdraws all the air out of an item giving it a sponge-like effect (an olive for instance). Then depressurise the chamber and the liquid fills the void that the vacuum has sucked out. This can be replaced with a liquid (vermouth works well with an olive).

Progressive drink creations, in my opinion, is here to stay at least in some shape or form. It definitely adds an extra dimension to a bartender's repertoire and has fundamentally changed the possibilities of cocktail drinking experiences for guests. In the last few years, and with the revival of the classic cocktail and the speakeasy bar, venues have sprung up all over the world using progressive techniques to put a fun and modern spin on your classic and contemporary drinks.

The evolution of drink making has meant that people can still approach the classics but in a more fun and innovative manner.

It's very important when creating progressive drinks or experimental cocktails that the guest has some point of reference. Some of the best creations I have seen or made have drawn inspiration from classic and contemporary cocktails. This should preferably be a drink that most people have tried before, such as an edible trio of classic cocktail sorbets such as a martini, mojito and cosmopolitan or a deconstructed Bloody Mary something people can relate and can all be portrayed in different ways and easily given a modern take or progressive makeover.

RECIPES

The following recipes can be recreated at home but needs some specialist equipment and ingredients.

I included them as if you do like to cook then all of these with the correct preparation are fun to create and can be construction relatively easily.

Polish Cappuccino

40 ml/1½ fl oz Polish vodka (see recipe below)
10 ml/⅓ fl oz Kahlua
10 ml/⅓ fl oz caramel foam (see recipe below)
double shot coffee

Shake and strain into a cappuccino cup.

Garnish with caramel foam and dark choc. Serve in a cappuccino cup and saucer with a sugarcane stick and teaspoon.

Vanilla Vodka

1. Slice two vanilla pods in half without splitting them completely.
2. Place in dishwasher for 2 cycles and let sit to cool for 10 minutes in between then store for 24 hours.
3. Taste to test if the infusion worked correctly.
4. Wrap white tape around the top of the bottle.
5. Strain vanilla pods out of bottle using a shaker and tea strainer.

Caramel Foam

1. Place three sheets of gelatin* in 250 ml/9 fl oz of cold water to soften.
2. Combine with 250 ml/9 fl oz of caramel syrup (Monin if possible).
3. Bring to the boil then simmer for 25 minutes.
4. Add water and gelatin to caramel mixture.
5. Using gloves, squeeze the gelatin to dissolve into the mixture.
6. Use a fine strainer to remove excess gelatin.

To Charge

1. Add 500 ml/17½ fl oz of caramel foam to creamer.
2. Charge with 2 cream bulbs.
3. Leave in the fridge for 2 hours to cool before use.

250-bloom count gelatin is fine and can be purchased in any good hospitality or chef store.

Rose Blossom Foam

45 ml/1½ fl oz Belvedere Orange
15 ml/½ fl oz Campari
30 ml/1 fl oz grapefruit juice
dash sugar syrup

Add all ingredients, shake and double strain into a martini glass.

Garnish with Rose Blossom Foam and rose petals.

Rose Foam
1. Place 3 sheets of gelatin in 250 ml/9 fl oz of cold water to soften.
2. Combine with 250 ml/9 fl oz of rose syrup (Monin if possible).
3. Bring to the boil then simmer for 25 minutes.
4. Add water and gelatin to sugar mixture.
5. Using gloves, squeeze the gelatin to dissolve into the mixture.
6. Use a fine strainer to remove excess gelatin.

To Charge
1. Add 500 ml/17½ fl oz of liquid to creamer.
2. Charge with 2 cream bulbs.
3. Leave in the fridge for 2 hours to cool before use.

Sugar Syrup
1. Mix two parts water to one part sugar.
2. Simmer on a gentle heat and stir until dissolved.
3. Let cool store in a sealed container and chill.

Citrus 'Air' Gimlet

70 ml/2½ fl oz Belvedere Citrus
15 ml/½ fl oz lime cordial
1 large scoop of lemon/lime sorbet
5 ml/⅙ sugar

Shake and strain into a small coupet glass. Garnish with a lemon and lime twist.

Citrus Emulsion

1. Place two bar spoons of sucros* into a bucket or jug and dissolve in 200 ml/7 fl oz water.
2. Add 200 ml/7 fl oz lemonade, 150 ml/5 fl oz lemon juice, 1.5 L/52 fl oz lime cordial.
3. Blend with the hand blender until there is a rich air on top. When a nice foam has been created by the hand blender scoop the bubbles off the top with a slotted spoon or sieve and place onto the drink.

*Sucros is an emulsifier and can be purchased from specialty cooking stores.

Edible Trio of British Classics

1 x Gin and Tonic
1 x Bloody Mary
1 x Shandy

Method
Build on slate

Glass
G and T: Presentation Spoon
Mary: Presentation Spoon
Shandy: Tall shot glass

Garnish
G and T: Small pinch of bicarbonate soda
Mary: Salt and pepper air
Shandy: Lemonade foam and side of salt chips

Edible Trio of British Classics Cont.

Jellies and Shandy Preparation

Gin and Tonic
1. Combine 3 teaspoons of agar agar and 250 ml/9 fl oz of water.
2. Place on the stove and bring the mixture to 86°C/186°F.
3. Combine 120 ml/4 fl oz Plymouth Gin, 400 ml/14 fl oz tonic water and sugar to taste.
4. Combine mixtures in a plastic container and refrigerate.

Bloody Mary
1. Combine 3 teaspoons of agar and 250 ml/9 fl oz of water (or 4 sheets of gelatine).
2. Place on the stove and bring the mixture to 86°C/186°F.

Combine 100 ml/3½ fl oz vodka, 650 ml/22¾ fl oz Homemade BBQ Mary Mix (see recipe p. 230), 100 ml/3½ fl oz tomato juice, lemon juice and soda to balance.
Combine the mixture in a plastic container and refrigerate.

Mini Shandy

1. Pour 40 ml/1½ fl oz of lager in a 60 ml/2 fl oz shot glass.
2. Top with lemonade foam (see recipe below).
3. Side of salt and vinegar crisps on the side.

Lemonade Foam

- Place 3 sheets of gelatin in 250 ml/9 fl oz of cold water to soften.
- Combine with 350 ml/12 fl oz of lemonade.
- Bring to the boil then simmer for 25 minutes.
- Add water and gelatin to sugar mixture.
- Using gloves, squeeze the gelatin to dissolve into the mixture.
- Use a fine strainer to remove excess gelatin.

To Charge

1. Add 500 ml/17½ fl oz of liquid to creamer.
2. Charge with 2 cream bulbs.
3. Leave in fridge for 2 hours to cool before use.

Edible Trio of American Classics

1 x Mini Martini with vermouth air
1 x Mojito Jelly
1 x Clover Club Sorbet

Method
Build on slate with 2 teaspoons

Glass
Martini: Presentation Spoon
Long Island Iced Tea: Presentation Spoon
Clover: Tall shot glass

Garnish
Martini: Vermouth air
Long Island Iced Tea: Lemon sugar
Clover: Grated orange

Mini Martini Jelly

1. Combine 3 teaspoons of agar agar and 250 ml/9 fl oz of water (or 4 gelatin sheets).
2. Place on the stove and bring the mixture to 86°C/186°F.
3. Combine 120 ml/4 fl oz 10 gin, 300 ml/10½ fl oz lemonade, 60–80 ml/2–2½ fl oz lemon juice, lemonade and soda to balance.
4. Combine mixtures in a plastic container and refrigerate.
5. Vermouth 'air' added when ready to serve.

Vermouth Air
1. Place two bar spoons of Sucro in 200 ml/7 fl oz of water.
2. Add 150 ml/5 fl oz Gomme and 200 ml/7 fl oz vermouth to taste.
3. Blend with the hand blender until there is a rich air on top.

Mojito Jelly
1. Combine 3 teaspoons of agar agar and 250 ml/9 fl oz of water.
2. Place on the stove and bring the mixture to 86°C/186°F.
3. Combine 120 ml/4 fl oz 10 Cane, 100 ml/3½ fl oz mint syrup, 60–80 ml/2–2½ fl oz lemon juice, with lemonade and soda to balance.
4. Combine mixtures in a plastic container and refrigerate.

Clover Club Sorbet
1. Combine 120 ml/4 fl oz gin, 100 ml/3½ fl oz lemonade and 250 ml/9 fl oz raspberry syrup and 60 ml/2 fl oz sugar syrup. Add 30 ml/1 fl oz lemon juice to balance.
2. Place in freezer to chill.
3. While chilling grind up 3 cups of dry ice.
4. Add to mixture slowly, sifting with a julep strainer, while hand blending until mixture is smooth but solid.

Breakfast Mojito

1 x tube Mojito toothpaste	Method
1 x beaker of Mojito mouthwash	Serve on a platter
1 x Amuse Bouche spoon with candied mint leaf and fizz powder	Glass Platter
1 x Injection of Rum	Garnish
1 x Frozen Shot Glass	2 lime slices

* Serve as per picture on page 141 and serve with Fizz powder lightly sprinkled on candied mint.

Mojito Toothpaste

1. Combine 3 teaspoons of agar agar and 250 ml/9 fl oz of water
2. Place on the stove and bring the mixture to 86°C.
3. Combine 120 ml/7 fl oz rum, 100 ml/3½ fl oz mint sugar syrup, 60–80 ml/ 2–2½ fl oz lemon juice, adding lemonade or soda to balance.
4. Combine mixtures in a plastic container and refrigerate.

Mint Sugar Syrup

1. To 1 litre/2 pints sugar syrup
2. Add 20–30 mint leaves.
3. Simmer on low heat for 20 minutes. Let sit and cool.
4. Fine strain, chill and store.

Mojito Mouthwash

1 litre/2 pints Mint Sugar Syrup

30 ml/1 fl oz blue food dye

600 ml/21 fl oz lemonade (to taste)

1. Steep 30–40 mint leaves in 1 litre/2 pints sugar for 2 to 3 hours. Stir each hour, shake well and stir then fine strain. To fast track you can simmer but this releases chemicals in the mint that dull the flavour).
2. Fill with water, stir and chill.

Fizz Powder

1. Add 600 g/21 oz icing sugar, 250 g/9 fl oz citric acid, 250 g/9 fl oz bicarbonate soda.
2. Shake and stir until ingredients are blended together.

Candied Mint

1. Pluck fresh mint leaf.
2. Dip in egg white.
3. Roll in fine sugar.
4. Place in dehydrator for 12–14 hours/or leave in a dry room on some baking paper and turn every 6 hours for 24 hours.

Margarita Ice Cream

100 ml/3½ fl oz dark rum
40 ml/1½ fl oz coconut cream
80 ml/2½ fl oz coconut liqueur
300 ml/10½ fl oz pineapple juice
80 ml/2½ fl oz sugar

Add above ingredients and chill.
While chilling grind up 3 cups of dry ice.
Add to mixture slowly while hand blending until sorbet texture is smooth but solid.
Keep frozen then scoop into small cone when serving.
Garnish with toasted coconut flakes.

Makes 500 ml/1 pint

British Summer Garden Martini

50 ml/1¾ fl oz gin
30 ml/1 fl oz apple juice
15 ml/½ fl oz chamomile syrup (see recipe below)
30 ml/1 fl oz cider syrup
3–4 cucumber pieces, peeled

Muddle fruit, add ingredients, shake and single strain. Serve in a coupette glass.

Serve on a turf platter with mini gardening tools, watering can with dry ice with a dash of water to make smoke. Floating cucumber with UK flag mist with cut grass essence.

*Set up as per photograph on page 148 and serve on a grass-bedded slate.

Chamomile Syrup

1. Place 7.5 L/15.8 pints water and 7.5 kg/16 lbs white graded sugar into the boiler and stir.
2. Place 6 teabags in mix.
3. Sit for 30 minutes (until a thick syrup is made) stirring regularly.
4. Taste to make sure there is a strong chamomile flavour.
5. Pour syrup into a container.

Cider Syrup

750 ml/24 fl oz good quality apple cider (Olde English)
½ cup fine sugar
1 tablespoon lemon juice
1 teaspoon ground cinnamon
2 tablespoon corn flour

To make the syrup, stir together the sugar, corn flour, and cinnamon in a saucepan.

Stir in the apple cider and lemon juice.

Cook over medium heat until mixture begins to boil; boil until the syrup thickens.

Cut Hay Sour

40 ml/1½ fl oz bourbon
30 ml/1 fl oz lemon juice
2 dashes bitters
20 ml/⅔ fl oz sugar syrup
½ Hay-infused Egg

Shake and strain into a tea cup and saucer with teaspoon and lemon slice.

Garnish with a lemon squeeze.

Edible Soil

125 g/4 oz caster sugar
125 g/ 4 ½ oz almond flour
75 g/ 2½ oz plain flour
50 g/1¾ oz unsweetened cocoa powder
pinch of salt
63 g/2 oz melted butter

Preheat the oven to 150°C/300°F.

Whisk all dry ingredients then stir in butter. Keep stirring to break up all clumps unti the mixture is smooth.

Spread mixture as thin as possible on baking tray with baking paper. Bake for 15 minutes.

Allow to cool and crumble any large remaining lumps. Store in an airtight container.

Firebucket!

160 ml/5½ fl oz buffalo trace
80 ml/2½ fl oz apricot brandy
2.25 litres/4.75 pints ginger beer
1 litre/2 pints lemondade
2 whole limes, cut in 6

Build and stir into a vintage firebucket (if you can get one!).

Garnish with 6 lime squeezes, 4 stripey straws and a dash of liquid nitrogen.

Caution: Please ensure 90 seconds is left before consuming to allow liquid nitrogen to disperse.

Serves 4

Smoked Chocolate Sazerac

60 ml/2 fl oz rye bourbon
15 ml/½ fl oz white cacao
2 dashes peychard
1 spoon sugar

Build and absinthe wash into an old fashioned glass over smoked ice.

Garnish with chocolate dust and chocolate smoke.

Smoked Bacon and Maple Syrup Manhattan

60 ml/2 fl oz maker's bacon-washed bourbon
1 tablespoon Cinzano Rosso
1 tablespoon Noilly Prat
1 tablespoon maple syrup
1 tablespoon angostura bitters

Add ingredients, stir. Add ice, stir and strain into a chilled martini glass.

Garnish with a maraschino cherry (sunk) and a speared maple-spiked crispy candied bacon.

Bacon-washed Bourbon

1. Pour 90 ml/3 fl oz of melted bacon fat (per bottle of bourbon) into bottle of quality bourbon. Let sit for 6 hours then freeze for 8 hours.
2. Finely strain out the fat and it is ready to use.

Champagne and Strawberries Martini

40 ml/1½ fl oz vodka
20 ml/⅔ fl oz crème de fraise
4–5 fresh strawberries
10 ml/⅓ fl oz sugar syrup

Muddle strawberries and shake and strain into a chilled martini glass.

Garnish with Champagne Air (see recipe below) and a candied strawberry.

Champagne Air

1. Place two bar spoons of Sucro in 200 ml/7 fl oz of water.
2. Add 150 ml/5 fl oz Gomme and 250 ml/9 fl oz sparkling wine to taste.
3. Blend with the hand blender until there is a rich air on top.
4. Use a small wine bucket to mix.

Lipstick Bellini

20 ml/⅔ fl oz crème de violette
10 ml/⅓ fl oz rose syrup
top with Chandon

Shake and strain into a coupet glass.
Garnish with a lemon twist and lipstick smudge.

Strawberry Smokin Shake

45 ml/1½ fl oz vanilla-infused vodka
25 ml/¾ fl oz strawberry liquor
60 ml/2 fl oz vanilla-spiked milk
60 ml/2 fl oz strawberry puree
dash vanilla liquor

Muddle, shake and strain into a milkshake tin. Garnish with a tea strainer filled with dry ice, candied strawberry and pinch of vanilla sugar.

Gunpowder Plot

50 ml/1¾ fl oz Gunpowder-infused Gin (see recipe below)
10 ml/⅓ fl oz Fernet Branca
10 ml/⅓ fl oz spiced syrup
3 dashes dandelion bitters
20 ml/⅔ fl oz lemon juice
1 egg white
5 ml/⅙ gunpowder tea
15 ml/½ fl oz sugar

All Spice Syrup
750 ml/24 fl oz sugar syrup
10 cloves
10 star anise
3 cinnamom sticks
1 split vanilla bean

Firstly, make the All Spice Syrup by putting all the ingredients in a small saucepan and simmering for 20 minutes. Cool then store.

Combine remaining ingredients, shake and strain. Serve in a small vintage martini.

Garnish with a lemon twist, smoking cloche, a pile of gunpowder (tea), bonfire twigs and the Union Jack.

Gunpowder-infused Gin
1. Combine 4 teaspoons of gunpowder tea into 1 bottle of Plymouth gin.
2. Add 6 lemon twists.
3. Place through glasswasher twice.
4. Let sit for at least 48 hours.

Nitro Martini

100 ml/3½ fl oz gin or vodka
30 ml/1 fl oz dry vermouth
200 ml/7 fl oz LN2
dash olive brine

Place the gin or vodka into a mixing tin (ensure to wear goggles and gloves at all times).

Pour in the dry vermouth, then the LN2. Add in the olive brine. Leave 1 minute then stir well until frozen. Store in freezer then serve on a canape spoon with an olive when ready.

Caution: Do not consume until left to rest in freezer for 30 minutes (must be store at -25 °C).

Nitro Punch

120 ml/4 fl oz citrus vodka
80 ml/2½ fl oz elderflower
1 bottle cider
300 ml/10½ fl oz apple juice
100 ml/3½ fl oz lemonade

Build in an antique punchbowl.

Add nitro and 6–8 lime squeezes and candied apple slices.

CHAPTER FOUR
Creating Your Very Own Home Bar

Creating Cocktails

Making great cocktails for dinner parties is not as common an occurrence as it should be in my opinion. Arriving to someone's home and being greeted with a well-made drink is impressive, and a great way to kick-start an evening.

Classic pairings such as a dry martini with oysters, a rum punch with some paté or cheese, a Pimms Cup with some light canapés all work well. It doesn't have to be complex but with a simple home bar set up and some basic liquors it is easier than many imagine.

In this chapter, I have listed some of the basic drink-making techniques, equipment and set-up for a home cocktail bar. This is entry-level stuff, great for beginners with easy-to-follow recipes.

BASIC DRINK-MAKING TECHNIQUES

There are seven basic cocktail making techniques.

Muddle

This technique is used in cocktails such as the Mojito, Caprioska and Caipirinha and requires the use of a flat-platted bar spoon or a muddler.
This technique involves pressing the ingredients to extract the juices and flavours from the fruit and any essential oils, to add a further dimension to your creation.
    For the best results, place the ingredients in the bottom of a Boston shaker and press with the bar spoon or muddler to extract the juices and flavours.

Build
This drink-making technique is as simple as it sounds with all the ingredients poured in order of the recipe, usually over ice. Drinks such as a Moscow Mule and a Dark and Stormy use this technique.

Shake and strain
Shaking and straining a drink normally requires the use of a shaker (either a three-piece or a two-piece Boston shaker) and a Hawthorn strainer. The idea of the 'shake and strain' is to chill the drink, mix ingredients and let the ice dilute the drink. Drinks that are shaken and strained include a Cosmopolitan, Mai Tai or Daiquiri.

Layer
Layered drinks such as a liqueur coffee or a shooter use this technique of floating or layering different liquor, liqueurs or additives such as cream or coffee. When layering alcohol be aware that the lower alcohol by volume (ABV) and higher sugar content liquids are placed on the bottom of the glass as they are more dense in structure. Ones with higher or similar ABV and less sugar are less dense so are floated on the top. For example a B52 shot is first Kahlua (ABV 20 per cent), then Baileys (17 per cent) then Grand Marnier (40 per cent).

Stirring
Many of the classic cocktails such as a martini and Manhattan are made with this technique. Simply stir your ingredients using a flat-platted bar spoon over ice for around 20 seconds in a mixing tin then strain into your chilled glass using either a hawthorn strainer or julep strainer to keep the ice behind.

Rolling

This is a technique for a drink that needs its ingredients fused together without too much dilution or adding too much air. This procedure is quite simple and involves the use of two Boston shakers, one with ice and one without, then pouring your ingredients from one to the other, including the ice. Repeat around 8–10 times then strain using a Hawthorn strainer. A Bellini or Bloody Mary could be made in this way.

Blending

Blended cocktails seem to go in and out of fashion. They were big business in the 1920s and 30s then almost became obsolete until the 70s and 80s then once more seem to dull in popularity but in the past few years appear to be coming back in. Many bars in the US, UK and Australia are now bringing the blenders back in and placing blended drinks back on their lists. Although due to the noise factor of many blenders you have to beware in smaller venues or restaurants.

For blending a cocktail, simply add all your ingredients into your blender, add two scoops of ice and blend until thick before serving. A good tip for blending drinks is to wait until you see a crease in the middle, it is the perfect viscosity; if there is a hole in the center of the liquid it is too aqueous.

BASIC EQUIPMENT FOR YOUR HOME BAR

Cocktail shaker
For shaking cocktails

Two-piece Boston shaker

Hampton or Parisian two-piece shaker

Three-piece shaker

Julep strainer
For straining many stirred cocktails, such as a martini or Manhattan—used to strain from the glass section of your Boston shaker. This bar tool grips the ice better than a Hawthorn, which is better suited when straining from the steel section of the shaker.

Hawthorn strainer
For straining cocktails

Fine strainer
This is used to strain out pips or pulp from a drink that can sometimes occur when muddling fresh fruit.

Flat platted bar spoon
For stirring, muddling, layering and measuring (the spoon is a standard 5 ml/⅙ fl oz in volume).

Jigger
A legal requirement in many bars around the world to measure your alcohol for both cocktails and mixed drinks.

Nip pourer
This fits into the end of a spirits bottle and helps give you extra control when pouring. You can either free pour—where a slow rhythmic count of 1-2-3-4 gives you around 30 ml/1 fl oz or pour into your jigger.

Chopping board and pairing knife
Both a good knife and chopping board are essential for cutting garnishes, preparing fruit and ingredients.

Ice
Ice is often a forgotten component but it is in fact one of the most important ingredients. It can be brought but I would recommend making your own. Simply freeze tap water into 3–4 plastic containers. Freeze until solid then remove for 20–30 minutes and freeze again, repeat 3 times. This 'triple freezing' process tightens the molecules in the water and makes it tough and a lot slower to melt and break down. Then chip to order. This technique is best when wanting to pour a quality liquor over, such as Scotch, bourbon or vodka.

Cocktail Glassware Examples

So much great glassware can be found around the world that it would be impossible to list all of my favourites.

Generally, I like LSA, Riedel and Waterford for premium and elegant products. Alternatively Plumm, Louis Bormioli and Schott Zwiesell are great for style, practicality and good value.

Martini glasses
These can be used for a Classic Martini, Daiquiri or Manhattan. Anything that is shaken and strained without ice.

Coupette glass
Originally used for champagne but now used more predominantly for many of the drinks above.

Highball glass
Can be used for any mixed drinks such as a gin and tonic or built cocktails such as a Sea Breeze, Moscow Mule.

Old fashioned or rocks glass
Can be used for mixed drinks also and also for cocktails such as an Old Fashioned or Negroni.

Shot glass
Can be used for sipping or shooting neat liquor or layered shooter.

Champagne
Can be used for champagne cocktails or champagne.

Beer/Pilsner
Can be used for beer-based cocktails or just beer and best stored chilled if possible.

Jam jar
Good for mixing up simple homemade cocktails and can add a fun and relaxed element to any home drinks or cocktail party.

Tin mug or can
As with the jam jar these can be used as a different serving vessel for Moscow Mules or Dark and Stormy's and also have the added benefit of being durable.

Tiki 'volcano' bowl
Can be used for some fun shared drinks such as rum-based punches. The volcano in the middle can be filled with overproof rum and lit so it flames!

Basic fruit
The following are good to keep at home or to purchase if entertaining:
- Lemons
- Limes
- Oranges
- Mint
- Apples
- Olives

Basic spirits
Some basic spirits worth stocking up on for your home bar include:
- Vodka
- Gin
- Scotch
- Gold tequila
- Light rum
- Dark rum
- Bourbon
- Vermouth

Basic liqueurs
- Cointreau
- Strawberry liqueur
- Apricot liqueur
- Chambord
- Dry vermouth
- Sweet vermouth
- Elderflower cordial (non-alcoholic)

Basic juices (fresh pressed if possible)
- Orange
- Lemon
- Lime
- Cranberry
- White grapefruit
- Pink grapefruit
- Apple juice
- Agave nectar

Ice
Always keep a good stock of ice whether it be bought in bag form or homemade as mentioned previously.

Garnishing your Creations

Lime squeezes

To cut these for your cocktail or mixed drink simply cut off the ends of your lime then roll 2–3 times before cutting into half then half again.

Rolling the lime releases the juice that is stored in the membranes ensuring you get more juice when it is squeezed into your drink.

Lemon squeezes

Prepare the same as the lime—to cut these for your cocktail or mixed drink simply cut off the ends of your lemon then roll 2–3 times before cutting in half then half again.

Lemon and lime twists

Twists are perfect for a variety of classic cocktails such as Martini's and Gimlets.

They can be produced using a sharp pairing knife. Alternatively, you can use a canelle knife where you simply draw around the circumference of the fruit and peel a twist from the skin.

Apple garnishes

To gain an effect similar to the one below use a sharp pairing knife and simply make a deep fan-shaped cut into the apple and then 'pop' out the fan shape and repeat for however many are required.

Mint sprigs

A mint sprig is the tip of a bunch of mint and can be used to garnish many cocktails including such classics as the Mojito and Mint Julep. It should not be confused with a mint leaf as these should be plucked off the bunch and can be used for muddling in cocktails.

Never over-muddle mint as the veins in the leaves contain chlorophyll and, when released, taste grassy or bitter. So always muddle or press mint lightly to avoid this.

Garnish skewers

Both plastic or wooden skewers can be used to display garnishes on drinks.

Olives can be speared for martini's and fruit can also be speared and placed on the rim of the glass, such as apples, strawberries and raspberries rather than just placed in a glass.

Simple Drinks Recipes to Create at Home

The recipes following can satisfy a variety of palates but are all quick and simple to fix up.

It is important to ensure preparation is done beforehand and you have all the correct ingredients to hand. Always stick as closely as possible to recipes to ensure consistency.

Classic Drinks

Classic Moscow Mule

**45 ml/1½ fl oz vodka
top with ginger beer**

An all-time classic that is both refreshing in the heat and warming in the cold. Light, spicy and easy to drink.

Top with homemade ginger beer (or bottled).
Build into a long glass over ice.
Garnish with a lime squeeze.

Dark & Stormy

45 ml/1½ fl oz dark rum
top with ginger beer

Like the Moscow Mule, just with Dark Rum, which adds a little bite.

Top with homemade ginger beer (or bottled).
Build into a long glass over ice.
Garnish with a lime squeeze.

Paloma

45 ml/1½ fl oz Tequila (Reposado if possible)
60 ml/2 fl oz freshly squeezed pink grapefruit juice
15 ml/½ fl oz fresh lime juice
10 ml/⅓ fl oz agave nectar

The name means 'dove' and it is a light, long, cool and refreshing twist on a Margarita.

Top with bottled or canned grapefruit soda.
Build into a long glass with a salt rim.
Garnish with a pinch of salt and a lime squeeze.

Oriental Breeze

45 ml/1½ fl oz orange-infused vodka
30 ml/1 fl oz lychee liqueur
60 ml/2 fl oz grapefruit juice
10 ml/1 fl oz lime juice
dash Bitters

A long and cool twist on a Sea Breeze—good with spiced food or cheese.

Build and stir into a highball glass with ice. Garnish with a lime squeeze.

Lemongrass Martini

60 ml/2 fl oz vodka
2–3 finely chopped lemongrass
20 ml/⅔ fl oz lemon juice
10 ml/⅓ fl oz dry vermouth
15 ml/½ fl oz sugar syrup

A great light-flavoured Martini, great on a hot summer's day or with Thai food or even Chinese.

Muddle lemongrass then shake and fine strain. Garnish with a lemongrass stick.

Sour Apple Martini

45 ml/1½ fl oz vodka
4–5 green apple chunks
2–3 lime wedges
20 ml/⅔ fl oz apple liqueur
15 ml/½ fl oz lemon juice
15 ml/½ fl oz apple juice

A good palate opener or could be served with light meats or fish.

Shake and fine-strain into chilled Martini glass. Garnish with an apple slice speared with a skewer.

Sake Cucumber Martini

45 ml/1½ fl oz vodka
2–3 pieces of fresh cucumber
10 ml/⅓ fl oz sake
60 ml/2 fl oz apple juice
10 ml/⅓ fl oz Sauvignon Blanc

Light and refreshing—good as a pre-dinner drink before Thai food or sushi.

Muddle cucumber. Add ingredients then shake and fine strain. Garnish with floating cucumber slice.

Strawberry and Balsamic Martini

45 ml/1½ fl oz vodka
4 strawberries (hulled)
10 ml/⅓ fl oz balsamic vinegar
20 ml/⅔ fl oz fraise liqueur

Light and fruity with a well-balanced acidity from the balsalmic. Good after a meal or with canapes.

Muddle strawberries then shake and strain into a chilled martini glass.
Garnish with a skewered half strawberry.

Elderflower Collins

45 ml/1½ fl oz vodka
15 ml/½ fl oz elderflower cordial
30 ml/1 fl oz lemon juice
20 ml/⅔ fl oz sugar syrup

Long and light good with salmon, sushi or light meats.

Shake and strain all ingredients into an ice-filled collins glass then top with soda.
Garnish with lemon squeeze.

Diamond Geeza

40 ml/1½ fl oz averna
150 ml/5 fl oz Guinness
20 ml/⅔ fl oz sugar
⅔ dashes dandelion bitters
1 egg white

Shake all ingredients together well. Serve in a glass-footed mug. Dust with nutmeg.

Toffee Apple Fizz Martini

40 ml/1½ fl oz vodka
10 ml/⅓ fl oz butterscotch liqueur
10 ml/⅓ fl oz caramel liquor
60 ml/2 fl oz fresh pressed apple juice

Shake and fine strain into a martini glass and garnish with a candied apple and mini toffee apple.*

*Place thin sliced apple into dehydrator for 12 hours.

Hibiscus Martini

50 ml/1¾ fl oz vodka
25 ml/¾ fl oz hibiscus syrup
1 dash sugar syrup
15 ml/½ fl oz lime juice

Shake and strain into a martini glass.
Garnish with a pinch of vanilla salt, pinch of sea salt and hibiscus flower.

Peach Bellini

20 ml/⅔ fl oz white peach puree
top with Spanish cava

Slightly sweet with a dry finish this bellini is great for a pre-dinner tipple.

Add puree first then slowly add cava and stir together into a chilled champagne glass.
  Garnish with a peach slice.

Citrus Ginger Mojito

45 ml/1½ fl oz citrus vodka
4–5 pieces of mint
15 ml/½ fl oz ginger syrup (see page 239)
10 ml/⅓ fl oz lime juice
2–3 pieces of lime

A great spiced twist on the classic. Perfect on a summer's night, served with light meats or seafood such as oysters or salmon.

Build and muddle the mint with lemonade. Serve long over crushed ice.
  Garnish with a mint sprig and a skewered slice of peeled ginger.

CHAMPAGNE FIXES

Champagne Breakfast

10 ml/⅓ fl oz citrus vodka
15 ml/½ fl oz limoncello
135 ml/4½ fl oz sparkling wine
1 tablespoon marmalade

Cleansing and with complex flavors from the limoncello and marmalade, this is good with seafood and oysters.

Add all ingredients except marmalade into shaker then shake and strain into a champagne flute and top with sparkling wine and the marmalade.

Garnish with an orange twist.

Champagne Citrus Mojito

5 lime wedges
6 mint leaves
2 barspoons raw sugar
dash mint syrup
25 ml/¾ fl oz citrus vodka

Good with canapés or as a pre-dinner drink.

Muddle lime, mint, sugar and syrup in a highball glass.

Add alcohol, stir well and top with crushed ice. Top with sparkling wine.

Garnish with a mint sprig and lime wedge.

Raspberry Bellini

20 ml/⅔ fl oz raspberry puree
dash sugar syrup
½ glass champagne

Fresh sweetness from the raspberries is balanced with the dryness from the sparkling wine this could be served pre-dinner or even served in a shorter old-fashioned glass post dinner.

Add puree first then slowly add champagne and stir together into a chilled champagne glass.
Garnish with a speared raspberry.

PUNCHES AND SANGRIA'S

Lemongrass and Mango Sangria

40 ml/1 ½ fl oz Amaretto
80 ml/3fl oz mango juice
60 ml/2 fl oz lemongrass syrup
½ bottle unoaked chardonnay
1 mango, peeled and sliced
2 lemongrass sticks, cut into 2 in pieces
2-3 scoops ice cubes
150-250 ml/5-9 fl oz lemonade or soda

Perfect to be placed in the middle of the table for a canapé-style get together as it is so light and refreshing it can go with either light meats or seafood.

Blend the liqueur, juice, syrup and wine.
Add mango pieces and lemongrass.
 Add ice cubes.
 Add lemonade to taste.
 Serve in a red wine glass with 6 slice of mango and 1 stick lemongrass and a wooden spoon.
 Ice on the side.

Vodka Orange Cooler

120 ml/4 fl oz Belvedere orange
90 ml/3 fl oz Campari
150 ml/5 fl oz cranberry juice
20 mls/⅔ fl oz lime juice
20 ml/⅔ fl oz sugar syrup

As above but without the spice and another layer of flavour with the orange.

Build in a 1.5 litre carafe or decanter with ice then top with equal parts soda and lemonade.

Garnish with orange, lime and ginger slices.

Pink Grapefruit Summer Sling

1.5 litre/3 pints jug

90 ml/3 fl oz vodka
60 ml/2 fl oz campari
60 ml/2 fl oz ginger liqueur
100 ml/3½ fl oz pink grapefruit
60 ml/2 fl oz blood orange juice

Slight spice from the ginger mixes well with the slight tartness from the pink grapefruit and blood orange. This is good for a barbecue or social get-together.

Top with soda and lemonade then add 2–3 scoops of ice.

Garnish with orange, lime and ginger slices.

'Smokin' Apple Punch

120 ml/4 fl oz citrus vodka
80 ml/2½ fl oz apple liqueur
60 ml/2 fl oz chamomile tea
400 ml/14 fl oz apple juice
300 ml/10½ fl oz lemonade

A light and fun 'party punch' as the smoking aspect is always a good party piece of photo opportunity. Nice, light and easily quaffable.

Build the drink in a punchbowl. Add 3 scoops of ice and 1 apple ice block. Place dry ice inside a tea leaf holder and place under warm water until smoking then drop into the punch.

Garnish with 6–8 apple slices and lime pieces.

* Use caution when using dry ice and never ingest.

Tinto de Verano

500 ml/17½ fl oz pinot noir
100 ml/3½ fl oz sparkling water
200 ml/7 fl oz sparkling pink grapefruit
60 ml/2 fl oz cranberry juice
top with soda and lemonade

'Tinto De Verano' literally means 'red wine of summer' in Spanish.

It is also sold in local supermarkets and along with calimocho (red wine and coke) is the preferred tipple of the locals while sangria is normally that of the tourists.

Build into a 1-litre carafe and 1 scoop of ice.

Garnish with 2 cucumber slices, 3 lime and lemon wheels and 3 grapefruit wheels.

Serve with short glasses.

Classic Spanish Sangria

400 ml/14 fl oz pinot noir/Sauvignon Blanc
60 ml/2 fl oz Cointreau
30 ml/1 fl oz lemon juice
30 ml/1 fl oz lime juice
top with equal amounts of lemonade and soda

Nice balance of flavours in this all-time classic—great with seafood or paella or Charcuterie meats.

Build into a 1-litre carafe and ½ scoop of ice. Garnish with 2 lemon wheels, 2 lime wheels, 3–4 grapes and 3–4 pieces of apple. Serve with iced wine glasses.

Twisted Sangria

300 ml/10 ½ fl oz pinot noir/sauvignon blanc
30 ml/1 fl oz Cointreau
30 ml/1 fl oz cognac
200 ml/7 fl oz orange juice
100 ml/3½ fl oz grape juice
top with ginger beer

Another great twist on the classic sangria—lighter and with a slight spiced finish of ginger beer.

Build into a 1-litre carafe and ½ scoop of ice along with 6–8 strawberries pieces. Serve with ice wine glasses and napkin

Garnish with 2 lemon wheels, 2 lime wheels, 3–4 grapes, 3–4 pieces of apple and strawberries.

Spanish Limonata

30 ml/1 fl oz lemon juice
60 ml/2 fl oz Galliano
45 ml/1½ fl oz sugar syrup
½ bottle pinot noir
2 lemons, sliced
1½ peaches, sliced
150–250 ml/5–9 fl oz lemonade or soda
4–6 frozen peach slices
2–3 scoops ice cubes

A light, more approachable twist on the classic sangria— not quite so dry and packed with a lot more flavour.

Blend juice, liqueur, syrup and wine.
    Add lemons and peach pieces.
    Add lemonade to taste.
    Serve each red wine glass with 3 pieces peach, 3 orange slices (quartered), 3 lemon slices (quartered) and a wooden spoon.

Mexican 'Ponche'

90 ml/3 fl oz rum
100 ml/3½ fl oz black tea
50 ml/1¾ fl oz orange juice
60 ml/2 fl oz grape juice
300 ml/10½ fl oz pineapple juice
20 ml/⅔ fl oz sugar syrup
Top with soda and lemonade to taste

This can be served either hot or cold (as below) with ice and is often served as a celebratory drink for birthdays or weddings with many using their own secret family recipes. The bitterness of the black tea, balanced with the sweetness of the Rum and juices make for a refreshing well balanced punch. Spices such as cardamom and cinnamon can be added if served hot.

Build into a 1-litre carafe and ½ scoop of ice. Serve with ice wine glasses and drinks coasters.

Garnish with 2–3 plum quarters, 2–3 orange slices and 4–5 grapes.

Mulled Wine

Serves 4–6

1 bottle (750 ml/24 fl oz) red wine (Cabernet Sauvignon)
1 orange, peeled and sliced (reserve peel to add zest to taste into pan)
125 ml/4 fl oz brandy
10–12 cloves
¾ cup honey or sugar
4 cinnamon sticks (broken)
1 teaspoon fresh or 2 teaspoons ground ginger
pinch of allspice

Many countries claim to have invented mulled wine. The heating and spicing of wine leads back to the Romans as far back as the first century. There are many variations in the UK, Netherlands, Germany as well as the ski fields of Austria and Switzerland were it is served to warm you after a ski run—or sometimes even before! The following is a more English variation.

To make the perfect cup of mulled wine, combine all ingredients in either a large pot or a slow cooker. Gently warm the ingredients on low to medium heat (avoid boiling), for 20–25 minutes. Leave until wine is steaming and serve.

'Smoke and Fire' Tiki Punch

120 ml/4 fl oz dark rum
80 ml/2½ fl oz apricot brandy
200 ml/7 fl oz pineapple juice
80 ml/2½ fl oz passionfruit puree
2 dash bitters
10 ml/⅓ fl oz sugar syrup
250 ml/9 fl oz lemonade

Another great party punch, this time a little heavier with rum and the addition of fire!

Build into a tiki punchbowl and stir. Add ice then light the volcano. Before serving, drop in a tea strainer filled with dry ice to add smoking effect.

Garnish with a mint sprig and 3 striped straws and drop overproof rum into volcano then light to flame.

Pimms Jug

180 ml/6 fl oz Pimms
Top with 250 ml/9 fl oz
ginger ale and lemonade.

The all-time UK classic and the cornerstone of garden parties, polo and tennis matches since the 1970s and a legendary summer tipple in the UK. Gin can be added if an extra kick is required!

Build into large 2-litre jugs with ice. Build into a 1.5 litre glass pitcher with ice.

Garnish with cucumber, orange, mint and strawberry. Serve in an old-fashioned glass with mint

Champagne Negroni

120 ml/4 fl oz gin
120 ml/4 fl oz Campari
120 ml/4 fl oz Sweet Vermouth
100 ml/3½ fl oz soda top with sparkling wine

A long refreshing and simple twist on the Negroni. Perfect with a charcuterie plate or oysters.

Build and stir into a 1 litre carafe and fill it half with ice.

Garnish with 2 pieces of limes/lemons/oranges.
Serve with old-fashioned glasses and lemon and orange slices.

Mandarin Punch

150 ml/5 fl oz orange vodka
60 ml/2 fl oz Campari
400 ml/14 fl oz ruby red grapefruit juice
150 ml/5 fl oz orange juice

A nice dry pre-dinner or canapé-style punch. Very light and easy to drink! Good with any light meat or canapé.

Build and stir into a 1-litre carafe, half filled with ice. Garnish with 3 lime squeezes, 3 lemon squeezes and 2–3 pieces of blood orange and serve with old-fashioned glasses.

Passionfruit and Red Grapefruit Punch

45ml/1½ fl oz Gold Tequila
10 ml/⅓ fl oz pomegranate juice
10 ml/⅓ fl oz Cointreau liqueur
60 ml/2 fl oz ruby red juice
30 ml/1 fl oz passionfruit pulp

Slightly dry and tart but a very light and refreshing punch the sweetness of the Cointreau is balanced well by the tartness of the pomegranate and ruby red juice.

Pour over ice cubes and build into a jug. Garnish with passionfruit pulp.

Aperol and Grapefruit Sour

45ml/1½ fl oz vodka
15 ml/½ fl oz Aperol
Top with sparkling grapefruit/soda mix from Siphon.

Vanilla Ice Cubes
200 ml/7 fl oz vanilla syrup (see page 244)
200 ml/7 fl oz lemonade
50 ml/1¾ fl oz water
dash lemon juice

A sort of Negroni-style mix but not so dry, with more depth of flavour for those who find a Negroni a little dry.

Pour over vanilla-flavored ice cubes (see recipe following) then build or stir into an old-fashioned glass.

Garnish with a lime squeeze.

Pour into the ice tray and freeze. Place into a glass then top with half pink grapefruit juice and half soda.

For vanilla ice cubes, fill fill a 500 ml/1 pint bottle with the ingredients. Pour into ice cube trays and freeze.

HOMEMADE RECIPES

Homemade Spiced Cherry Cola

30 ml/1 fl oz Pepper Vodka
Top with Homemade Cherry Cola (see recipe page 233)
dash lime juice

Build into a jam jar inside a brown paper bag. Garnish with a lime squeeze and a twist of black pepper.

Homemade Gin and Tonic

45 ml/1 ½ fl oz gin
Top with homemade tonic (page 234)

Pour into an old-fashioned glass over chipped ice.
Garnish with a lime or lemon squeeze.

Homemade Moscow Mule

45 ml/1 ½ fl oz vodka
Top with homemade ginger beer (page 237).

Pour into a tall glass or tin camping mug over chipped ice.
Garnish with a lime squeeze.

Homemade Dark and Stormy

45 ml/1 ½ fl oz dark rum
top with homemade ginger beer (page 237)

Pour into an old-fashioned glass or tin camping mug over chipped ice.
Garnish with a lime or lemon squeeze.

Homemade Cherry Cuba Libre

45 mls Light Rum
top with Homemade Cherry Cola (see recipe page 233)

Build in a highball glass and garnish with a lime squeeze and twist of black pepper.

Homemade 5 Berry Daiquiri

50 ml/1¾ fl oz rum
10 ml/⅓ fl oz homemade lime cordial (see page 242)
60 ml/2 fl oz five-berry mix (see page 239)
dash sugar syrup
2 scoops ice

Place into a blender and blend with 2 scoops of ice until thick. Pour into a coupet glass.

Garnish with three-speared berries and a lime squeeze on side of glass.

Homemade Lavender French 75

10 ml/⅓ fl oz gin
dash homemade lavender syrup
dash lemon juice
top with sparkling wine

Top with sparkling wine and build into a champagne flute.

Garnish with a twist of lemon.

Lemongrass Bellini

15 ml/½ fl oz lemongrass syrup
dash Cointreau

Build into a champagne flute and top with sparkling wine.
Garnish with a stick of lemongrass.

Hibiscus Bellini

15 ml/½ fl oz hibiscus syrup
dash Cointreau

Build into a champagne flute and top with sparkling wine.
Garnish with a twist of orange or edible flower.

Mint and Vanilla Cooler

30 ml/1 fl oz white rum
dash Cointreau or other orange liqueur
dash lime juice
dash vanilla syrup
10 ml/⅓ fl oz sugar syrup
2–3 drops vanilla extract

Build into a jam jar over ice. Stir well then top with chilled soda water.

Garnish with mint sprig.

Homemade Lime and Nettle Gimlet

60 ml/2 fl oz gin
10 ml/⅓ fl oz homemade lime cordial
dash nettle syrup

Shake very well with ice then fine strain and pour into a chilled martini glass.

Garnish with a twist of lime.

Homemade BBQ Bloody Mary

35 ml/1¼ fl oz vodka
Top with Homemade Bloody Mary Mix (see page 241)

Shake well with ice then pour into a soup or bean can (be careful of sharp edges).

Garnish with a twist of black pepper, twist of salt, crisp bacon and 2 cherry tomatoes.

HOMEMADE SYRUPS AND RECIPES

Homemade Cherry Cola
7-day shelf life

2 split vanilla pods
2 teaspoons citric acid
2 tablespoons dry lavender
120 ml/4 fl oz fresh orange juice
160 ml/5½ fl oz cherry juice
4 dash biters
30 ml/1 fl oz lemon juice
200 ml/7 fl oz raspberry puree
1 cup sugar
1 x 355 ml/12 fl oz can cola
½ x 355 ml/12 fl oz can soda water

Place all the ingredients in a pan and simmer for 30 minutes. Let the liquid cool then finely strain and add coke and soda to taste.

Homemade Tonic

7-day shelf life

5 cups water
2 cups chopped lemongrass
2 teaspoons cinchona bark flakes
zest of 1 orange/lemon/lime
8 twists black pepper
1 teaspoon all-spice berries
½ teaspoon citric acid
½ salt
1 cup agave

Combine all the ingredients and simmer or boil for 20 minutes.

Cool, strain and add ½ cup more of agave to taste.

Store then carbonate when required.

Homemade Ginger Beer
7-day shelf life

4 kg/8.8 lbs ginger
4 litres/8½ pints water
600 g/21 oz honey
4 tablespoons brown sugar
4 bay leaves

Peel ginger and slice very thinly.

Combine with water, honey, sugar and bay leaves in a large pot.

Bring to the boil then simmer for 30–40 minutes.

Store and strain into soda siphons as needed, charged with 2 soda bulbs.

Keep refrigerated (makes 5 litres/10 pints).

Lavender Syrup
10-day shelf life

5-7 little fresh lavender flowers
½ cup sugar
½ cup water

Bring ingredients to a boil. Reduce heat and simmer for about 5 minutes or until the sugar dissolves. Stir as needed to keep the sugar from sticking to the bottom of the pan.

Transfer to an airtight container or large jam jar and let chill in the fridge. Strain out the lavender after an hour and let it chill.

Lemongrass Syrup
10-day shelf life

1 cup sugar
1 cup water
2 stalks of fresh lemongrass

Remove the outer layer of lemongrass stalks and discard. Cut the remaining lemongrass into pieces.

Mix equal parts water and sugar same as simple syrup in a pot.

Add lemongrass.

Bring to boil and then turn down heat.

Simmer for 20–25 minutes.

Cool then and pour in a jar, date and store.

Homemade 5 Berry Syrup

10-day shelf life

1 cup frozen blueberries/ raspberries/ strawberries/red currants/blackcurrants
60 ml/2 fl oz agave nectar
80 ml/2½ fl oz sugar syrup
3 tablespoons caster/ superfine sugar

Place in a blender and blend until in a syrup then store.

Ginger Syrup

10-day shelf life

1 cup sugar
1 cup water
1 kg/36 oz fresh ginger

Remove the outer layer of ginger skin and discard. Cut the ginger into pieces, around 1 cm/¼ in thick.

Mix equal parts water and sugar same as simple syrup in a pot.

Add ginger.

Bring to a boil and then turn down the heat.

Simmer for 20–25 minutes.

Cool and pour in a mason jar. Date and store.

Homemade Bloody Mary Mix

Makes 3 Litres (10-day shelf life)

2 litres/4 pints tomato juice
8 tablespoons BBQ sauce
6 dashes of tobacco sauce
6 tablespoons Worcestershire sauce
2 tablespoons Cajun spice
8 twists of black pepper
2 pinches of salt

Mix all together in a large bowl.
Blend all with hand blender for 1–2 minutes.
Chill, label and store.

Homemade Lime Cordial

(12-day shelf life)

- 12 limes
- 5 cups water
- 5–6 cups sugar
- 2 teaspoons citric acid
- 1½ teaspoons tartaric acid

Peel lime to gain zest then mix with sugar, citric and tartaric. Boil water then add these to them and simmer for 20 minutes. Stir until all dissolved then add lime juice and continue to simmer for 10 minutes. Strain and store.

Hibiscus Syrup

7 day shelf life

- 4 tablespoons hibiscus
- 300 ml/10½ fl oz sugar
- 200 ml/7 fl oz water

Simmer for 20 minutes then let cool. Finely strain then label and store chilled.

Nettle Syrup

7 day shelf life

4 tablespoons nettle leaf
300 ml/10½ fl oz sugar
200 ml/7 fl oz water

Simmer for 20 minutes then let cool.
Finely strain then label and store chilled.

Espresso Foam

2 litre/4 pints

10 gelatine sheets–high bloom count
400 ml/7 fl oz caramel syrup
180 ml/6 fl oz sugar syrup
90 ml/3 fl oz espresso

Soak the gelatine for 15 minutes.

Combine the caramel topping and sugar syrup. Add in the espresso.

Add all combined ingredients to the soaked gelatine and simmer in a saucepan for 20 minutes then let cool.

To charge, add 500 ml/17½ fl oz of liquid to creamer gun. Charge with 2 cream bulbs.

Leave in fridge overnight to cool.

Sugar Syrup

makes 5 litres. 14-day life shelf

5 litres/10 pints water
7.5 kg/16½ lb white graded sugar

Place water and sugar into a large saucepan and bring to the boil, stirring constantly.

Sit for 20 to 30 minutes (until a thick syrup is made) stirring regularly.

Pour syrup into a container and store.

Vanilla Syrup

7 day shelf life

1 litre/2 pints water
1 kg/36 oz white sugar
12 split vanilla pods

Place water and sugar into a large saucepan and bring to a boil. Stir.

Place the split vanilla pods into mixture.

Remove from the heat and let sit for 20 to 30 minutes (until a thick syrup is made) stirring regularly.

Taste to make sure there is a rich vanilla flavour.

Pour syrup into a airtight container and chill until ready to use.

DESSERT COCKTAILS

These are great recipes that can be served during or after dinner, at a cocktail party or more casual drinks. For example, the espresso martini a great way to start an evening while the Vanilla passion is a popular way to finish.

Vanilla Passion

45 ml/1½ fl oz vanilla-infused vodka
15 ml/½ fl oz vanilla liqueur
¼ vanilla pod
60 ml/2 fl oz passionfruit
dash lemon juice
dash apple

Shake and strain into a chilled martini glass. Garnish with passionfruit pulp.

Citrus Sorbet Gimlet

70 ml/2½ fl oz citrus vodka
15 ml/½ fl oz lime cordial
2 large spoonfuls of sorbet

Shake and strain well into a coupette glass. Garnish with a lemon and lime twist.

La Premiere

50 ml/1¾ fl oz popcorn-washed rum (see recipe below)
1 bottle of vodka
top with bottled coke

Pour the popcorn-washed rum into the bottle of vodka. Let sit for 6 hours. Freeze for 8 hours.

Fine strain out the fat. Build into a classic coke glass and top with coke. Serve garnished with caramelised popcorn and a lime squeeze.

Popcorn-washed Rum

4 large tablespoons clarified butter
2 pinches of salt
1 bottle light rum

Add the butter and salt to the bottle of rum. Let sit for 6 hours then freeze for 8 hours. remove then fine strain out the butter into a clean bottle. Add a pinch of salt to the bottle and serve.

Espresso Martini

45 ml/1½ fl oz vanilla vodka
10 ml/⅓ fl oz caramel
2 espressos
10 ml/⅓ fl oz kahlua
dash sugar syrup

Shake and strain into a coffee glass.
Garnish with Espresso Foam (see page 243), chocolate and sugarcane stick and saucer and chocolate shaved chocolate.

Affogato Espresso Martini

45 ml/1½ fl oz dark rum
15 ml/½ fl oz kahlua
10 ml/⅓ fl oz maple syrup
2 shots espresso
dash sugar syrup
1 scoop vanilla ice-cream

Shake well as needs foamy head.
Garnish with shaved choc and an extra scoop of vanilla ice cream if you wish.

Raspberry and Lemongrass Martini

30 ml/1 fl oz raspberry puree
30 ml/1 fl oz Belvedere pure vodka
15 ml/½ fl oz sake
15 ml/½ fl oz framboise
15 ml½ fl oz lemon juice
15ml/½ fl oz lemongrass syrup

Shake and double strain into a martini glass. Garnish with lemongrass skewer.

Vanilla and Cognac Martini

4 5ml/1½ fl oz cognac (infused with vanilla pods)
20 ml/⅔ fl oz sauvignon blanc
60 ml/2 fl oz pineapple juice
dash of sugar syrup

Shake and strain into a martini glass with a vanilla sugar rim and ½ a vanilla pod.

CHAPTER FIVE
Food and cocktails

CHAPTER 5

Food and Cocktails

Forward and Recipes By Danny Russo

Danny Russo specialises in modern Italian cuisine, reworking classic recipes to create a combination of traditional flavours with modern style.
He draws on his childhood in southern Italy and later youthful memories in Australia of family and friends congregating in the kitchen. Memories steeped in the marriage of flavours, aromas and laughter from shared meals with friends and family. Food and wine are a way of life and the corner stone of conviviality for Danny. They are the principles by which he develops and executes his culinary magic. That philosophy is grounded in *La Bella Figura*. More than just beauty and aesthetics, it is respect and the correct behaviour - the deep seated etiquette of the table and everything that makes that possible.

His professional experience was honed in kitchens in Australia and across Europe, including London, Rome and Marseille. Classically trained, he draws from the culture and flavours of the world with his heart wrapped in the tricolours of the Italian flag.

Danny was awarded both a Chef's Hat, and 'Best Formal Italian Restaurant' in the *Restaurant and Catering Association Awards* for three consecutive years at L'Unico Restaurant (Balmain, Sydney).

Then at Lo Studio in Sydney' Surry Hills he was awarded a Chef's Hat, 'Best Italian Restaurant' and 'Best New Restaurant Nationally', elevating the restaurant to one of Sydney's premier Italian Restaurants. Lo Studio was also named in the *Conde Nast Traveler* "Hot Tables" list among an elite group of 82 new

restaurants worldwide identified as having a unique confluence of great food, outstanding service, and sophisticated style. The magazine described Danny as "one of Sydney's most inventive chefs" who has "developed a style best described as New Italian-Australian fusion".

While at the highly acclaimed The Beresford Hotel in Surry Hills, Danny was featured twice in the *New York Times*, as well as receiving rave reviews in *Vogue Entertaining and Travel, Sydney Morning Herald, Time Out, The Daily Telegraph and The (Sydney) Magazine*. *Gourmet Traveller* described Danny's food as "some of Sydney's most Intriguing Italian food", with The Beresford having "the edge in terms of a pure eating experience". His most recent consulting work at The Old Library in Sydney's beachside suburb of Cronulla, has seen his cooking and influence earn the new establishment accolades from *The Sydney Morning Herald*, *The Daily Telegraph* and *The Sunday Telegraph* in an unprecedented week-long stream of glowing reviews. His work at Neutral Bay's White Hart has produced crowd-pleasing menus with bar food that has set a new standard.

"Matching wine with food is second nature to me," he says. "The pin-pointing of complementary dishes for cocktails is an alchemy that is based on basic flavour profiles but allows for fabulous bending of rules and the subtle introduction of sympathetic taste sensations that can produce thought-provoking and rewarding combinations."

COCKTAILS AND FOOD RECIPES

Cheese, Speck and Truffle Toasties

40 ml/1½ fl oz milk
160 g/5½ oz grated provolone cheese
50 g/1¾ oz store-bought black truffle salsa
8 slices thick cut (1.5 cm/2 in) bread
50 g/1¾ oz butter
4 thin slices of speck

Serves 4

These are a great idea for a social gathering. These go well with a beer, glass of white wine or even an Aperol Spritz.

Heat milk and cheese together over a low heat and stir until the cheese and milk have blended together. Remove from heat and allow to cool.

Spread a thin layer of truffle salsa on one side of the bread, then add a slice of speck and spread on a thin layer of the cheese mix. Place the other piece of bread on top. Butter on both sides, place in a non-stick pan and cook until golden brown.

Serve with a slice of shaved black truffle.

Aperol Spritz

45 ml/1½ fl oz aperol
top with sparkling wine

Build into a highball and pour over ice.
Garnish with a mint sprig and orange slice and stir.

Truffle Egg, Beetroot, Cauliflower, Asparagus and Parmesan

Serves 4

4 truffle eggs, soft poached
8 white asparagus
300 ml/10½ fl oz cauliflower puree
300 ml/10½ fl oz beetroot puree
100 g/3½ oz parmesan crisps

CAULIFLOWER PUREE
½ medium-sized cauliflower, cut into small pieces
1 clove garlic, finely sliced
50 g/1¾ oz butter
½ onion, finely chopped
50 ml/1¾ fl oz extra virgin olive oil
250 ml/9 fl oz vegetable stock
salt and pepper

PARMESAN CRISPS
100 g/3½ oz parmesan, grated

BEETROOT PUREE
3 medium-sized beetroots

To make the cauliflower puree, sauté the garlic and onion in butter and oil in a saucepan on medium heat, until transparent. Add cauliflower. Turn to simmering heat and cook for a further 5 minutes. Add water and allow to cook for approximately 20 minutes. By this stage the cauliflower should be soft enough to puree. Remove from heat and allow too cool. Once cool, place the cauliflower in a food processor until very smooth. Season and set aside.

Spread a thin layer of grated parmesan cheese in a large non- stick tray and heat gently until it melts and fuses, taking care not to brown it. The cheese should be soft, not crisp. Remove from heat, cut into desired shapes or allow too cool and then crush.

Wash and place beetroots in a pot and fully submerge them in cold water. Add the sugar and vinegar, place on the stove to boil for about 25 minutes. Check by using a skewer. Once the skewer can easily be inserted into the beetroot it is ready to take off the heat and strain. Once cooled, peel and cut into small pieces.

In a saucepan on a medium heat, sauté the garlic and onion in butter and oil until transparent. Add the beetroot and Marsala and cook for a further 5 minutes, allowing the Marsala to reduce by half. Add the stock and allow to cook for approximately 15 minutes. By this stage, the beetroot should be soft enough to puree. Remove from heat and place

60 ml/2 fl oz white wine vinegar
20 g/2/3 oz brown sugar
water (enough to cover the beetroots)
1 medium-sized brown onion, peeled and roughly diced
1 garlic clove, thinly sliced
50 ml/1¾ fl oz marsala
80 g/2½ oz unsalted butter
100 ml/3½ fl oz vegetable stock
salt and pepper

Truffle Poached Eggs
4 truffle eggs
1.5 litres/52 fl oz water
60 ml/2 fl oz white wine vinegar

White asparagus
8 white asparagus, peeled and blanched
30 g/1 oz butter unsalted
¼ bunch chives, finely diced
salt and pepper

the beetroot in a food processor and blitz until very smooth. Season with salt and pepper and set aside.

Truffle poached eggs
Add the water to a saucepan, add the vinegar and bring to the boil. Break the egg into a small ramekin or bowl and tip it gently into the pan, at the point where the water is bubbling. Repeat this process with the other eggs and cook for about 2 minutes. Using a slotted spoon, lift out the first egg and press the outside edge lightly to check if it is properly cooked.

As soon as the egg is cooked to your liking, remove. Trim the edges with a small knife to make a neat shape if required.

White asparagus
Cut the asparagus into 6 cm/3 in pieces.

In a saucepan on medium heat, melt the butter and add the asparagus, season with salt and pepper. Remove from the heat and add the chives.

Duck Liver Pate with Marsala Jelly, Cornichons and Grissini

500 g/1 lb fresh duck livers
250 ml/9 fl oz milk
100 ml/3½ fl oz water
2 eshallots, finely sliced
1 garlic clove, crushed
freshly grated nutmeg
6 sprigs of thyme
2 bay leaves
75 ml/2½ fl oz brandy
75 ml/2½ fl oz port
75 ml/2½ fl oz Madeira
150 g/5 oz butter, melted
2 whole eggs
100 ml/3½ fl oz cream

Serves 4

These little treats are perfect as a canapé on its own or as part of a canapé degustation using any of the other recipes listed here. A Pale Ale or Dark Ale would go with these well as well as a Negroni.

Preheat the oven to 120°C/250°F.

In a bowl, soak the duck livers in milk and water with a good pinch of salt for 2 hours. This will help to reduce bitterness. Then drain and wash the livers and drain again.

In a saucepan, add the sliced eshallots, garlic, sprigs of thyme, bay leaves, brandy, port and Madeira. Heat gently, reducing down until you have about 100 ml/3½ fl oz remaining and then pass through a fine sieve.

Using a high-powered food processor, place the livers, the reduction and the melted butter and puree until a fine and smooth texture appears.

Then add the eggs and puree for a further 3 minutes. Then slowly add the cream and puree for another 1 minute. Adjust the seasoning, with salt and pepper.

Push the mixture through a fine sieve.

Line a terrine mould with greaseproof paper that has been lightly oiled on both sides. Pour the mix in; it should come just to the top and cover with a lid.

Duck Liver Pate cont.

MARSALA JELLY
500 ml/1 pint water
55 g/2 oz caster/superfine sugar
4 sheets gelatin (soaked in water and drained)
250 ml/9 fl oz marsala wine
muslin cloth

Bake the terrine in a water bath for 50 minutes. To check it is done, the parfait should be 63°C/145°F in the centre. Test with a thermometer.

Once cooked, remove from the oven and remove the terrine mould from the water bath. Allow to chill, then refrigerate overnight.

To make the marsala jelly, put water and sugar into a saucepan and leave to soak for 5 minutes, then heat slowly, until dissolved. In a separate saucepan, reduce the marsala by three-quarters. Then add the liquid from the other saucepan and allow too reduce by one-quarter. Strain through double muslin and allow to cool. Add the gelatin and mix.

To serve, spoon some of the parfait into a piping bag and three-quarter fill the desired mould, cover with the marsala jelly and return to the fridge until set.

Place on a small slate plate serve with cornichons and grissinis.

Negroni

30 ml/1 fl oz gin
30 ml/1 fl oz sweet vermouth
30 ml/1 fl oz campari

Build into an old-fashioned glass over ice and stir well.

Garnish with 2 orange twists.

Zucchini Flowers with Porcini and Ricotta

100 g/3½ oz fresh ricotta
40 g/1½ oz dried porcini mushrooms, soaked in water for 2 hours, drained and chopped
1 tablespoon porcini paste
1 tablespoon parsley, chopped
50 g/1¾ oz parmesan cheese, grated
salt and pepper
12 zucchini flowers
For the egg wash:
150 g/5 oz plain/all-purpose flour, for coating
4 whole eggs

In a bowl, add the ricotta, chopped porcini mushrooms, porcini paste, parsley, parmesan and mix until the ingredients have blended. Season to taste.

Place the mixture into a piping bag. Open the zucchini flower and fill it three-quarters full with the mixture, then twist and turn the top of the flower to secure the seal.

Roll the flowers individually into the flour, then the beaten eggs and then the flour again. Once the flowers are coated, deep-fry until golden brown. Drain, season and serve.

Pork Belly Donuts

200 g/7 oz plain/all-purpose flour
100 g/3½ oz cornflour
pinch of salt
300 ml/10½ fl oz water warm
10 g/1/3 oz dried yeast
1 egg
300 g/10½ oz pork belly

In a mixing bowl, add the flour, cornflour and salt and mix together. Place the warm water in a measuring jug and mix with the dried yeast. Once the yeast has dissolved, add the liquid to the flour mixture and mix.

Add the egg and mix until a smooth a smooth paste has formed, cover with cling wrap and allow to rest at room temperature for 2 hours before using.

Cut the pork belly pieces into 2 cm cubes. Dip the pieces in the batter and deep-fry until golden.

Remove and coat with sea salt and maple syrup.

Ocean Trout 'Puttanesca' Crostini

240 g/8½ oz sashimi-quality ocean trout
16 micro heirloom cherry tomatoes
8 lemon-marinated white anchovies
8 confit garlic cloves (see recipe below)
8 thinly sliced, toasted bread, crushed
4 sprigs of fennel tops
30 g/1 oz baby capers, well rinsed and crispy fried
50 ml/1¾ fl oz extra virgin olive oil
30 g/1 oz sea salt

GARLIC CONFIT
150 ml/5 fl oz olive oil
8 garlic cloves, peeled and washed

Serves 4

These perfect casual bites are great with a rose wine or crisp pilsner.
Alternatively, try a Red Wine Spritzer.

Place oil in a small saucepan over medium-low heat. Add the garlic and cook over a very low heat until soft, about 1 hour (do not brown).

Tomatoes
Make a small incision on the bottom of the tomato and blanch quickly, refresh in cold water. Pat dry, lift the skin to the top of the tomato and deep-fry the tomato skin until crispy, season and set aside.

To assemble
Place the cut ocean trout on a plate, surround with the cherry tomatoes, crispy capers, confit garlic, crushed toasted bread, lemon-marinated anchovies and the fennel tops. Season with sea salt and drizzle with extra virgin olive oil.

Red Wine Spritzer

150 ml/5 fl oz light red wine (pinot noir or similar)
top with soda water

Build into a tall glass. Garnish with an orange, lemon and lime slice.

Oysters in Pastry

2 bunches flat-leaf parsley
salt and pepper
10 large spinach leaves
10 oysters
3 sheets phyllo pastry
1 egg
extra virgin olive oil

Wash the parsley, eliminate the stems and blanch the leaves for a few seconds in boiling water. Refresh in an ice bath, drain, dry and puree in a food processor. Season with salt and pepper.

Wash the spinach and blanch in boiling salted water for a few seconds. Drain, refresh in ice water and spread the leaves on a towel to dry.

Spread each spinach leaf with a little parsley puree, top with an oyster and add another small dollop of parsley puree. Wrap the oysters in the spinach leaves, taking care that the parcels are closed.

Cut the phyllo dough into 10 uniform squares, brush the edges with the beaten eggs, top each with an oyster, fold over the dough and press the edges to seal. Fry in oil and serve.

Lamb Sliders with Rosemary and Mint

Makes 8 sliders

500 g/1 lb lamb mince
1 teaspoon salt
cracked black pepper
1 teaspoon fresh mint, finely chopped
1 teaspoon fresh rosemary, finely chopped
1 clove garlic, finely chopped
100 g/3½ oz onion, finely chopped
50 ml/1¾ fl oz olive oil
8 slider buns
8 beetroot slices
100 g//3½ oz feta cheese
80 ml/2½ fl oz harissa sauce

Place lamb in a mixing bowl and add the salt, pepper, mint, rosemary, garlic and onion and mix well until the all the ingredients have combined. Then form into patties and pan-fry until cooked.

Slice the buns in half, place a slice of beetroot on the base of a bun, then add the lamb patty, feta and a dollop of harissa.

Pork Belly With Balsamic Onions

Serves 4

PORK BELLY
1 kg/36 oz pork belly, skin on
50 ml/1¾ fl oz olive oil and pinch of sea salt

BALSAMIC ONIONS
500 g/1 lb baby pickling onions, peeled and left whole
100 ml/3½ fl oz balsamic vinegar
500 ml/1 pint vegetable stock (hot)
50 g/1¾ oz honey
30 ml/1 fl oz olive oil

These tasty morsels can be enjoyed with a nice crisp Pilsner, Lager or try with a Margarita.

Preheat the oven to 150°C/300°F.

Using a sharp knife, score the skin of the belly being careful not to cut all the way through to the meat. Place the pork belly on a wire rack (skin side up) in a tray and in the fridge. Leave it overnight allowing the skin to dry.

Rub in the oil, then salt the pork skin generously, making sure to rub the salt into the skin and cuts.

Place it in a preheated oven for 30 minutes at 150°C and then increase the temperature to 180°C/350°F for another 30 minutes. Then increase it to 220°C/420°F for a further 15 minutes until the skin is crisp and the deepest amber gold in colour.

Cut into 3 cm x 4 cm cubes.

Trim the onions of any remaining peel and hairy bits.

Pork Belly Cont.

In a saucepan over medium heat, add the olive oil and brown the onions, turning them over, until they are golden in colour.

In a mixing bowl, mix the vinegar and honey.

Add the mixture to the onions and cook for 5 minutes on a medium–high heat, stirring continuously.

Add the hot vegetable stock, to just cover the onions in the saucepan, cover the saucepan with a lid and cook on a slow heat for 45 minutes, adding a little more stock gradually as needed.

Margarita

45 ml/1 ½ fl oz Gold Tequila
10 ml/⅓ fl oz Cointreau
30 ml/1 fl oz freshly squeezed lime juice
10 ml/⅓ fl oz sugar syrup

Shake and strain well into a short glass over ice with a sea salt rim.

Garnish with a lime squeeze.

Pork Scratchings

1 piece of pork skin, in from the belly with some underlying fat left on
salt

These moorish nibbles are probably best enjoyed with a glass of Shiraz or Pale Ale. But a Lagerita also pairs perfectly with the richness of the pork

Place the pork skin on a wire rack (skin side up) in a tray and in the fridge. Leave it overnight to allow the skin to dry.

Preheat the oven to 150°C/300°F.

Salt the pork skin generously, making sure to rub the salt into the skin.

Then place it in the preheated oven for 1½ hours until thoroughly crisp and the deepest amber gold in colour. Turn the skin over and cook the other side. Allow it to thoroughly dry out and crisp up.

Remove from the oven and cut or snap into short strips.

Lagerita

45 ml/1½ fl oz Gold Tequila
10 ml/⅓ oz Cointreau
20 ml/⅔ fl oz agave syrup
2–3 lime pieces
dash lime juice
top with lager

Place first 5 ingredients into a pilsner glass and muddle well.
Then add ice and top with lager and stir again.
Add a pinch of sea salt and lime squeeze as a garnish.

Pork Belly Sliders with Pickled Cabbage

Serves 6

Pork Belly

2 kg/4 lb 6 oz pork belly, female, boneless
2 litres/4 pints pork or chicken stock
2 teaspoons fennel pollen
2 teaspoons sea salt
50 g/1¾ oz Dijon mustard
1 tablespoon maple syrup

Pickled Cabbage

1 small savoy cabbage
60 ml/2 fl oz maple syrup
125 ml/4 fl oz white vinegar
60 ml/4 fl oz olive oil
1 teaspoon coriander seeds, toasted
½ teaspoon mustard seeds, toasted

Preheat the oven to 150°C/300°F. Rub the fennel pollen and sea salt into the rind of the pork belly. Place on a wire rack in a baking tray, skin side up, and add the liquid, not over the meat. Cover and cook for 4 hours until soft.

Allow to cool before slicing.

For the pickled cabbage, remove the tender leaves from the cabbage and steam until cooked but still a bit crunchy. Cool in ice water.

Whisk the maple syrup, the white wine vinegar and the olive oil in a bowl. Add the toasted coriander and mustard seeds. Drain the steamed cabbage and add to the pickling liquid. Refrigerate for at least an hour, or overnight.

To assemble, combine the Dijon mustard and maple syrup to taste.

Grill, roast or pan-fry slices of pork belly.

Split the brioche buns in half and toast the cut side.

Assemble the sliders with the brioche buns, pickled cabbage, pork belly and maple mustard.

Bruschetta l'Inferno

Serves 4

500 g/1 lb fresh black mussels
50 ml/1¾ fl oz olive oil
100 ml/3½ fl oz white wine
1 large red capsicum/bell pepper
1 large yellow capsicum/bell pepper
1 sprig thyme
chilli flakes, to taste
2 garlic cloves, whole (for the mussels)
2 garlic cloves, sliced thin
40 g/1½ oz tomato paste
1 orange, cut into segments
4 thick bread slices, toasted
10 basil leaves

Clean and beard the mussels. Place a large pot over high heat and add the oil and garlic. Once the garlic has coloured, add the mussels and wine and cover with a lid. Cook until the mussels have opened, about 5 minutes.

Using a slotted spoon, remove the mussels leaving the liquid behind. Allow the mussels to cool and remove the meat from the shell and set aside. Discard the shells.

Meanwhile, reduce the mussel liquid by half.

In a separate pot, sauté the sliced garlic, thyme and chilli flakes. Then add the capsicums and allow to cook for 10 minutes. Then add the tomato paste and cook for a further 5 minutes. Add the strained mussel liquid into the capsicum mix and allow too cook for a further 5 mins. Once all the ingredients have combined remove from the heat and allow too cool.

Then add the mussels and orange segments to the capsicum mix, season with salt and pepper and serve on toasted bread and drizzle with oil.

Roast Almonds, Green Sicilian Olives and Lavender

Serves 4

200 g/7 oz fresh almonds, skin on
20 ml/⅔ fl oz extra virgin olive oil
1 pinch of sea salt
100 g/3½ oz green Sicilian olives
1 sprig lavender
1 L/36 fl oz water, to blanch almonds

Try an Almond Old Fashioned with these or a pinot noir or pilsner.

Preheat the oven to 160°C/320°F.

Place a saucepan on the stove with water on high heat and bring to a boil. Add the almonds and allow to blanch for 30 seconds. Drain and place on a kitchen towel. Immediately wrap the almonds in the kitchen towel and begin to rub, this loosens the skin. Using your fingers, remove any skin still on the almonds.

Transfer the almonds to a mixing bowl and add the oil and salt, toss to coat evenly, then transfer to a non-stick baking tray.

Place in the preheat oven, stirring the almonds every 2 minutes until evenly coloured. This process should take 15 minutes. Once golden brown, remove from the oven and transfer to a paper lined tray to cool completely, remember to remove the almonds from the hot tray or they will continue to cook and risk the chance of burning the almonds.

Once completely cool, place the now roasted almonds in a bowl, mix with the green Sicilian olives, lavender and serve.

Almond Old Fashioned

60 ml/2 fl oz Gold Tequila
10 ml/⅓ fl oz Amaretto
20 ml/⅔ fl oz agave nectar
3–4 dashes of orange bitters

Build all ingredients over ice into an old-fashioned glass.

Add half ice and all ingredients and stir 8–10 times. Add rest of ice stir 3–4 times and finish with a dash of Gold Tequila and dash of orange bitters.

Garnish with 2 orange twists.

Roast Peppers Filled with Eggplant, Cous Cous and Olive Dressing

Serves 4

8 red bell peppers/capsicums
100 g/3½ oz cous cous
20 g/⅔ oz pine nuts
20 g/⅔ oz currants
20 g/⅔ oz black olives, seeded and thinly sliced
100 ml/3½ fl oz warm vegetable stock
10 ml/⅓ fl oz extra virgin olive oil
1 medium-sized eggplant, sliced (1 cm/¼ in rounds) grilled and finely diced
1 tablespoon parsley, finely chopped
Pinch of dried oregano
Salt and pepper

A glass of Rosé, Rosé Spritz or Pilsner

For the Roast Bell Peppers

Preheat the grill to 200°C/400°F.

Using a pastry brush, coat each red bell pepper evenly with oil. Make sure to coat inside the folds of each capsicum.

Arrange the peppers on a roasting tray and place on the highest rack in the oven.

Keep a watchful eye on the peppers. When dark patches begin to appear on the capsicums, remove the tray from the oven. Using tongs carefully turn each pepper over. Once all the peppers are turned, return the tray to the oven.

When the peppers are blistered and darkened all over, remove from the oven and place them into a large bowl. Cover the bowl with plastic wrap making sure that it is sealed air-tight all the way round. The steam from the hot peppers will loosen the skins.

Allow the peppers to cool for about 20 minutes before pulling the stems out of each pepper.

Hold one end down on a flat surface and gently peel the skin off. The skin should peel off fairly easily.

Using your knife, trim the top of the peppers and scrape off any of the membrane and seeds that remain.

Roast Peppers Cont.

For the filling

Place cous cous in a bowl and toss through with olive oil. When coated, add the warm vegetable stock and cover bowl with cling wrap for 10 minutes to allow the cous cous to absorb the moisture. After 10 minutes, remove the plastic wrap from the bowl and, using a fork, run through the cous cous to loosen and allow to the grains to separate. Then add the remaining ingredients and season to taste. Using a spoon, fill the peppers with the mix and place in 180°C/350°F pre-heated oven. Once heated through, assemble and serve.

Rose Spritz

150 ml/5 fl oz Rose
Soda

Build over ice into a highball glass. Garnish with a lemon twist.

Spiced Rubbed Lamb Ribs

Serves 4

4 Lamb Riblets

Spice Mixture

½ cup brown sugar
1 tablespoon ground cumin
1 tablespoon ground ginger
1 tablespoon garlic powder
1 tablespoon onion powder
1 tablespoon ground allspice
2 tablespoons smoked paprika
1 tablespoon ground white pepper
1 tablespoon rosemary powder
2 tablespoons salt

The perfect accompaniment for this would be a pinot noir, pale ale or Moscow Mule

Lamb Ribs

Preheat the oven to 160°C/320°F.

In a mixing bowl, place all the spices together and mix thoroughly.

Using a sharp boning knife, trim the lamb ribs of any excess fat and cut into individual ribs.

Sprinkle the spice mixture liberally over the lamb ribs and set aside for 1 hour in the fridge allowing the flavours to combine and develop.

Remove the ribs and place in a non-stick baking tray. Add water in the tray, allowing to fill no more than 1 cm/¼ in high, cover with foil and allow to cook in the preheated oven for 1½ hours.

Once cooked, remove from the oven and allow too cool. Roll the ribs in flour and fry until crispy and serve with sea salt.

Moscow Mule

45 ml/1½ fl oz vodka

Top with ginger beer.
Build into a tall glass or camping mug over ice.
Garnish with a lime squeeze.

Cheese Pralines with Caviar

250 g/9 oz taleggio
150 g/5 oz robiola
100g mascarpone
salt, to taste
grated nutmeg, to taste
1 egg
150 g/5 oz plain/flour
150 g/5 oz dry white breadcrumbs
oil, for frying
caviar, to serve

Cut the taleggio into very small pieces and combine in a bowl with the the robiola and the mascarpone. Beat with a fork until smooth and creamy. Season with salt and grated nutmeg.

Line a small tray with plastic, pour in the cheese mixture and smooth the surface about 2.5 cm/1 in thick, allow to cool for several hours in the cooler.

Cut the firm cheese into uniform cubes. Lightly flour, dip in egg wash, breadcrumbs and fry until golden brown. Serve with caviar.

Crispy Chicken Wings

4 eggs
500 ml/17½ fl oz buttermilk
1 kg/36 oz chicken wings, rinsed and jointed
cottonseed oil, for frying
700 g/1 lb 9 oz plain/all-purpose flour
200 g/7 oz panko crumbs
10 g/⅓ oz ground white pepper
5 g/¼ oz dried rosemary
15 g/½ oz cayenne pepper
10 g /⅓ oz sea salt
10 g/⅓ oz garlic powder
10 g/⅓ oz ground ginger
10 g/⅓oz Szechuan seasoning, for dusting

Mix eggs in a bowl and whisk in the buttermilk until smooth. Mix in the chicken wings, cover, and refrigerate for at least several hours.

Heat the deep fryer to 180°C/350°F.

Combine the remaining ingredients in a large mixing bowl until evenly blended.

Remove each chicken wing, letting the buttermilk mixture drip off. Pack in the breading, then gently shake off any excess breading. Repeat to coat all of the chicken wings.

Fry in batches in the hot oil until the meat is no longer pink at the bone and the breading is crispy, about 10 minutes. Turn the wings frequently to ensure even cooking. Drain on a paper towel-lined plate. Sprinkle with additional salt and Szechuan seasoning to taste, and serve.

'The Little Golden Delights'

Potato Scallops

Ingredients

Serves 4 to 6
400 g/14 oz small potatoes
220 g/8 oz self-raising/self-rising flour
1 teaspoon sea salt
1 sprig rosemary, chopped just before serving
200 ml/7 fl oz soda water
oil, for deep-frying
extra flour, for dusting
1 lime, cut in quarters

A fantastic accompaniment for the little delights would be Pale Ale or try a Lavender French 75.

Method

Peel and wash potatoes. Cut into thin slices, about 3 mm thick and place on absorbent paper towels and dry well.

Sift flour and salt into a bowl and make a well in the centre. Gradually add the soda water, mixing to a fairly thick coating batter (thick enough that it coats your finger). Beat until smooth and free of lumps.

Place a large pan with oil on the stove over medium heat (test the heat of the oil with a small amount of batter; you don't want the oil to be smoking).

Coat potato slices lightly with extra flour and shake off excess.

Dip each slice into prepared batter, making sure potato slices are well covered. Drain excess batter from each slice before frying.

Deep-fry potato slices, a few at a time, until lightly golden in colour. Remove from oil and drain on absorbent paper. Repeat this process until all the potato scallops are finished.

Increase the heat of the oil slightly and re-fry the potato scallops, re-fry until golden brown in colour. Drain again, sprinkle with sea salt, chopped rosemary and enjoy.

Lavender French 75

10 ml/⅓ oz gin
dash homemade lavender syrup
dash lemon juice
top with sparkling wine

Build into a champagne flute and garnish with a twist of lemon.

Truffle and Parmesan Arancini

500 g/1 lb arborio rice
50 g/1¾ oz onion, brunoise
1 garlic clove, thinly sliced
1.5 litres/52 fl oz chicken stock, hot
3 tablespoons truffle paste
50 ml/1¾ fl oz white wine
200 g/7 oz grated parmesan
1 egg yolk
100 g/3½ oz butter
For the breading:
200 g/7 oz plain/all-purpose flour, for dusting
300 g/10½ oz dry breadcrumbs
6 whole eggs
2 litres/70 fl oz olive oil, for deep frying
100 ml/3½ fl oz aioli

Arancini pairs perfectly with wheat beer, shiraz or a whiskey-based cocktail such as a Blood and Sand.

In a saucepan over medium heat, sauté the onions and garlic in butter. Cook until the onions are transparent. Add the rice and allow too toast the rice for several minutes. Once the rice is toasted add the white wine and allow the wine to reduce by half. Then gradually pour in the hot stock, a ladle at a time. Repeat this method until the rice is cooked al dente.

Once cooked, remove from the heat and add the parmesan and truffle paste and mix through. Season with salt and pepper and spread out on flat tray to cool. Once cooled, add the egg yolks and mix through the rice and correct the seasoning.

Wet your hands to stop the rice from sticking, then take a golf ball sized ball of rice in palm of your hand and roll into smooth balls. Repeat this process until the rice is finished and place the rice balls on a tray.

Place the flour and the breadcrumbs into separate shallow bowls. Place the whole eggs into a mixing bowl, and using a fork beat the eggs together.

Truffle Arancini Cont.

Dip each rice ball into the flour and coat, dust off any excess flour, then dip into the egg wash allowing to drip off any excess liquid, then roll into the breadcrumbs, making sure they are completely covered in crumbs and pressing them lightly to make sure the crumbs stick.

Place the oil in a saucepan deep enough to hold the amount of oil on the stove over medium to high heat until the temperature reaches 180°C (if you don't have a thermometer, test the oil by putting a few breadcrumbs in the oil – if they sizzle gently the oil is ready to use)

Put several of the arancini in the oil at a time, careful not to over crowd as it will lower the temperature of the oil and won't colour evenly. Fry the arancini for about 4 minutes until they are golden brown all over. Drain on paper towels, season with sea salt and serve hot.

Blood and Sand

30 ml/1 fl oz whisky
30 ml/1 fl oz sweet vermouth
30 ml/1 fl oz fresh squeezed orange juice

Shake and strain all ingredients into a coupet glass. Garnish with a cherry and orange twist.

Vitello Tonnato Sliders

Serves 4

2 litres/70 fl oz veal stock
500 g/1 lb Veal Girello
(Veal Girello is a cut from the back leg, also known as 'salmon cut' or 'eye of round'
4 bread rolls
100 g/3½ oz mixed leaves

A good Cabernet Sauvignon, wheat beer or a Mint Julep would be perfect matches for these sliders.

Poached Veal

Bring stock to the boil, drop in the girello and return to the simmer. Switch off the heat and allow to return to room temperature. Then slice the meat thinly to serve.

Serve with a slice of shaved black truffle.

TONNATO SAUCE
6 anchovy fillets, in oil
20 g/⅔ oz capers
2 hardboiled egg yolks
½ juice of a lemon
20 ml/⅔ fl oz white wine vinegar
220 g/8 oz tuna in oil, drained of oil
50 ml/1¾ fl oz veal braising liquid

Tonnato Sauce

Put the braising liquid in a blender, add the tuna, anchovies, capers, hard boiled egg yolks, lemon juice and vinegar and blend until the sauce is emulsified and velvety.

Using a bread knife, cut the bread rolls in half lengthways, place the sliced veal on the bottom, mixed leaves on top and a spoonful of the tonnato sauce and serve.

Mint Julep

10–12 torn mint leaves
60 ml/2 fl oz bourbon
15 ml/½ fl oz sugar syrup
top with a splash of bourbon

Build into a tin mug and muddle mint and sugar before adding crushed ice and stir 2–3 times. Garnish with a mint sprig and drizzle of bourbon.

Bacon, Bourbon, Caramel Popcorn

300 g/10½ fl oz bacon, diced
1 cup popcorn kernels
250 g/9 oz butter (the amount you'll need will depend on how much bacon fat you have)
400 g/14 oz brown sugar
6 tablespoons bourbon, divided
½ teaspoon sea salt
1 teaspoon baking soda
1 teaspoon vanilla
¼ teaspoon cayenne pepper

Place the diced bacon in a medium-sized frying pan over medium high heat. Cook the bacon for 7–10 minutes, or until it is quite crispy. Remove the bacon from the pan with a slotted spoon and reserve the bacon fat.

Pour 2 tablespoons of the bacon fat into a large pot over medium heat. Add 2–3 popcorn kernels and cover the pot. When you hear the first kernels start to pop add the remaining kernels all at once. Give the pot a shake and reduce the temperature to medium low. Continue shaking the pot occasionally until most of the popping has died down. Remove the pot from the heat. Pour the popcorn into 2 large bowls, making sure that no un-popped kernels get into the bowl.

Pour the reserved bacon fat into a 1-cup measuring up. Fill the rest of the cup with butter and then pour it into a medium-sized pot. Add the brown sugar, 4 tablespoons of the bourbon and the sea salt to the pot. Attach a sugar thermometer to the side of the pot and bring the pot to a boil. Stir the pot once then let it boil without stirring until the sugar thermometer reads 135°C/275°F (this will take approximately 4–5 minutes). When the sugar thermometer reads

135°C/275°F immediately remove the pot from the heat and stir through the baking soda, vanilla, cayenne pepper and the remaining 2 tablespoons of bourbon. Be careful at this point as the caramel will bubble up considerably and create a lot of steam.

Immediately pour the caramel over the popcorn, tossing the popcorn as you pour the caramel over it.

Toss the crispy bacon through the popcorn.

Preheat the oven to 135°C/275°F. Line two rimmed baking trays with parchment paper. Pour the caramel-covered popcorn evenly between the two trays. Bake the popcorn in the preheated oven for 15 minutes.

Remove the popcorn from the oven and let it cool completely before storing it in an airtight container.

Cured Ocean Trout with a Radish, Apple and Cress Salad

Serves 6+

1 teaspoon juniper berries
100 g/3½ oz salt
100 g/3½ oz sugar
50 ml/1¾ fl oz brandy
500 g/1 lb ocean trout (skin on)

Place the fish skin-side down onto a clean tray. Mix the berries, salt, sugar and brandy together until you get a thick slurry (add some water if necessary).

Pour the slurry all over the flesh of the fish to create a thick crust. Cover the tray in cling wrap and allow to cure for 10–12 hours.

Remove the fish from the tray and wash thoroughly under cold running water. Dry well with a paper towel and, using a sharp knife, cut the trout into paper-thin slices.

To make the salad, use a mandolin, slice the radish and apple at approx. 5mm thick. Cut the apple slices into little batons but leave the radish slices whole.

Season and dress the salad.

Arrange the sliced trout on the plate to cover the entire base.

Arrange the salad on top and garnish with the baby celery leaves and extra virgin olive oil.

Fried Calamari with Squid Ink Aioli

plain/all-purpose flour, for dusting
120 g/4 oz calamari, cleaned, cut into 5 mm rings
1 lemon, zest grated
10 g/1/3 oz parsley, chopped
cottonseed oil, for frying
salt and pepper

Put the flour in the bowl and toss the calamari in the flour until evenly coated. Place the floured calamari in a sieve and shake off any excess flour.

Place the calamari in a deep-fryer at 180°C/350°F and cook until golden brown. Drain well and place in a bowl lined with kitchen paper. Season, add parsley, grated lemon zest and serve.

DRINKS INDEX

VODKA

Affogato	250
Aperol and Grapefruit Sour	223
Black Russian	83
Bloody Mary	55
Blue Lagoon	48
Caprioska	93
Champagne and Strawberries Martini	158
Champagne Breakfast	203
Champagne Citrus Mojito	204
Citrus 'air' Gimlet	131
Citrus Ginger Mojito	202
Citrus Sorbet Gimlet	247
Cosmopolitan	89
Dry Martini	24
Elderflower Collins	195
Harvey Wallbanger	98
Hibiscus Martini	201
Home made Moscow Mule	225
Homemade BBQ Bloody Mary	230
Homemade Ginger Beer	237
Homemade Spice Cherry Cola	224
James Bond Cocktail	31
Lemongrass Martini	193
Mandarin Punch	221
Moscow Mule	94, 288
Nitro Martini	165
Nitro Punch	166
Polish Cappuccino	127
Pink Grapefruit Summer Sling	207
Prohibition Iced Tea	67
Raspberry Lemongrass Martini	251
Rose Blossom Foam	129
Sake Cucumber Martini	194
Smoking Apple Punch	208
Sour Apple Martini	194
Strawberry Balsamic Martini	195
Strawberry Smokin Shake	161
Toffee Apple Fizz Martini	199
Vesper Martini	81
Vodka Orange Cooler	205
White Russian	83

WHISKEY

Algonquin	45
Almond Old Fashioned	282
Blood & Sand	295
Fire Bucket	152
Manhattan	27
Mint Julip	105, 299
Old Fashioned	51
Sazerac	23
Trilby	49

GIN

Aviation	82
British Summer Garden Martini	146
Bronx	42
Champagne Negroni	220
Charlie Chaplain	62
Dry Martini	24
Edible trio of British Classics	132
Edible trio of American Classics	136
Gibson	28
Gimlet	21
Gunpowder Plot	16
Homemade Gin and Tonic	225
Homemade Lavender French	227
Homemade Lime and Nettle Gimlet	229
Lavender French	75, 292
London Fog	52
Long Island Iced Tea	97
Negroni	263
Ping Pong	59
Prohibition Iced tea	67
Singapore Sling	37
The Martinez	41
Twentieth Century Cocktail	60
Vesper Martini	83
White Lady	64

RUM

3 Dots & A Dash	102
Between the Sheets	82
Blackbeard's Ghost	110
Breakfast Mojito	140
Caprihina	101
Cuba Libre	32
Daiquiri	34
Dark & Stormy	192
Dr Funk	112
Homemade Cherry Cubre Libre	226
Homemade Dark & Stormy	226
Homemade Five Berry Daiquiri	227
La Premier	248
Long Island Iced Tea	97
Mai Tai	106
Mexican 'Ponche'	214
Mint & Vanilla Cooler	229
Mojito	79
Piña Colada	86
Planters Punch	92
Prohibition Iced Tea	67
Smoke and Fire Tiki Punch	217
Test Pilot	103
Zombie	85, 109

TEQUILA

Margarita	80
El Diablo	93
Long Island Iced Tea	97
Tequila Sunrise	103
Deconstructed Margarita	120
Margarita Ice Cream	145
Paloma	192
Passionfruit & Grapefruit Punch	222
Margarita	274
Lagerita	277

US $24.99
UK £16.99